Always the voice of reason.
    Philip Mayers, Mayers Recruitment

Hard hitting and provocative. A must read for teachers and educators who are willing to think.
    Charles Kovess, Kovess International

You are sincerely thanked for opening minds with these thought starters. You have also introduced unfamiliar words that need scrutiny and discussion.
    Charryce Nixon-Luke

Do enjoy reading your perspectives on education.
    Debi Slinger, Smarter Property Investing

Bravo! (You woke me up)
    Howard Hutchins, Speaker, Mentor, Strategist

I really enjoy your thought starters.
    Daniel Mundy, ANZUK Education

Always food for thought. Keeping us all on our toes.
    Michelle Saunders, Parent

Wow! What a great quote Cheryl: 'It would seem that human rights have outweighed what it is to be a responsible human.'
    Mel Philips, Enhanced Educational Solutions

I am in full agreement with your comments. I have letters written by my mother over 40 years ago sent from the UK. I also have 2 of her diaries where she left comments such as 'letter from Liz today' usually about a week apart. Lovely and very precious memories. Thank you for always sharing your thoughts.
    Elizabeth Smith, Joli Reading

Thank you for sharing with me all your articles this year. I have enjoyed everyone. I look forward to reading next year's articles.

    Jane Marshall, Special Needs/Pre-Service Teaching Coordinator

So true! You get stuck with what you are given when you send kids to school. Teachers need to be paid more, but teachers need to be graded too.

    Patricia Williams Hawke, Current Affairs Researcher

Thought Starters on Education

Reflect • Respond • Share • Act

Cheryl Lacey

For John and Margaret

Copyright © 2019 by Cheryl Lacey

All rights reserved. No part of this book may be reproduced, stored in a retrieval system, or transmitted in any form or by any means, electronic, mechanical, photocopying, recording, or otherwise, without written permission from the publisher.

ISBN: 978-0-6485282-1-0 (paperback)
ISBN: 978-0-6485282-0-3 (hardcover)

First Edition

CONTENTS

Foreword by Dennis Troedel KSJ ix

Introduction xiii

Chapter 1: Unions 1
   A Funding Discussion: Pencil It In! 2
   Playing the Trump Card: Uniting for Merit 4
   Schools: Who Needs Them? 6
   Strike One, You're Out!
   The Unions: A Blight on Public Education 9
   Propaganda, Infiltration, Legislation:
   Why Unions Should Stay Out of Classrooms 18

Chapter 2: Gender and Sexuality 23
   Watch Out for Women 24
   The Weight of Trust: Sex, School and Society . . . 27
   Is the Male Teacher an Endangered Species? . . . 33
   Remaining Abreast of Equality 35

Chapter 3: Funding and School Choice 37
   You Oughta Be Congratulated 38
   Exchanging Printed Paper for Effective Education
   Services: A Wise Choice? 40
   Positive Action: Adding Value to School Funding . 53
   Adding Value to Our Schools 57

Chapter 4: Genuine Parent Relationships . . . 61
   Genuine Partnerships 62
   The Highly Regarded Educator 64
   Hold Back the Creep 66

Trumping Australian Schools. 68

Challenging the Norm 73

Parents: Be Aware, Be Assertive, Be the Voice . . .75

Advocating for What's in Common 78

Parents Treated Like Rubbish 80

Power of the Big G. 83

Chapter 5: Authenticity 85

A Sprinkle of Difference. 86

Reality: Yours, Mine, Ours 88

To Be of Service 91

The Principal Act 93

To Guarantee Continued Freedom 96

Chapter 6: Pedagogy and the Teaching Profession 101

Can We Detect a Heartbeat?. 102

Pedagogy to Puppetry:
Who's Pulling the Strings? 105

Flushing Out Failure 108

Is Teaching Really a Profession? 111

Commitment to Capability 114

The 'Some' of Us 116

Evolution Instead of Revolution:
Thinking About Personalised Teaching 118

Chapter 7: English Language and Literacy . . 123

There's 'Something' About Education 124

Self-inflicted Digital Incarceration:

Be Careful What You Hope For 126
Raising Poor Spellers 129
Literacy, Technology and the 21st Century . . . 132
Moving Forward with Fundamentals 134
'Either-or' Means Everyone's a Loser 136
The Teaching of English: A Primary Concern . . . 139
Handwriting: Gone With The Wind 143
Who's Hijacking the English Language? 146
Essential Fundamentals. 148
Writing Slump in Australian Schools 150
What Are Our Children Really Worth? 153

Chapter 8: Politics and Schools 155

Political Correctness: Honestly? 156
The Historian in Each of Us 158
Are You Smarter Than a 12-year-old? 160
Discrimination: Discerning Difference 163
Faith in Morality 166
Safe Schools No More 169
The Servants of Hopes and Dreams 175
The Consequence of Freedom 178
Dental Decay: Something is Rotten
in the State of Victoria 181
What Is This Space We Call Place? 183

Foreword

When children become adults, earn an income, and begin to contribute successfully to society, how much of their success can be attributed to schools and how much to parents and others of influence?

Developing leadership potential, knowing how to compete and win, or lose graciously – provided the competition is fair – and learning to pick themselves up, and go on, are essential learning experiences – part of life's journey for young people.

Is a school responsible for providing these learning experiences?

Must schools provide sufficient knowledge and understanding, in terms of *why* they should, and *how* they might meet their own, their parents' and the community's expectations?

This raises another question. Are there sufficiently high levels and standards in the various faculties – such as

Thought Starters On Education

Mathematics, English, Humanities, and the Sciences – to provide this knowledge and understanding?

These questions, and many more, must be answered.

Education provided in Australian schools has undergone profound change since its introduction in the late 1700s. We no longer rely on chalk and slate; neither do we rely on publications approved of and distributed by governments of other nations. It's fair to say that, in recent years, electronic communications dominate.

With these changes and so many others, we must ask ourselves 'why' and 'how' do 21st century schools currently provide education? We must also ask ourselves how parents view the education Australian schools promise and/or provide, and whether or not it has value.

Over the last twenty years education has become a huge export earner for Australia, as many pupils come here from countries such as China, India, and Japan. This is a great thing in some ways, but have educators become lost, in terms of what education is really all about? Schooling is to prepare our youth for their life in society – as parents, leaders and, above all, good citizens in our community of tomorrow.

As a result of the evolution of education reform during the past 200 or more years, what has Australia achieved? And what has been compromised?

Foreword

One educationist in particular – Cheryl Lacey – has been asking many of these questions and has been at the forefront of drawing our attention to them.

Cheryl is an Australian-born parent of two daughters, an educationist, a Rotarian of note and a member of some ten societies and institutes. She has an impressive clientele, having worked with leaders in public, independent and denominational educational settings, Australian and international, covering early childhood, elementary, and secondary levels.

Over the years, Cheryl has been a strong advocate for 'agitating change in Australian education', and has published many books and articles, including *The Ultimate Parent Teacher Interview* – a two-volume guide for teachers and parents.

She also writes a weekly article, aptly titled *Thought Starters on Education.* Each piece aims to provoke discussion on current issues: union influence in schools; declining standards in English; dwindling pride in teaching training and professional standards; contradictions between State and Federal government values; funding; and the impact of home-school-work-family-life balance on all of us.

This book is the result – the first in what will be a series of compilations of Cheryl's *Thought Starters on Education.*

In your reading you will discover thought-provoking content that will have you do exactly what Cheryl intends: *reflect, respond, share and act* on her questions and her insights.

Thought Starters On Education

Through each piece you will also sense her commitment to schools, families, and the self-respecting, responsible, responsive and generous individuals who make up the Australian community.

—Dennis Troedel KSJ

Introduction

For centuries philosophers have sought answers to what it means to have a good education, and how education relates to life and life's purposes. We are still searching for those answers.

Today, researchers and governments continue to put forward ideas, strategies and solutions for the 'right' way to educate our young people. Most are motivated by the desire for genuine improvement; some pursue their own financial and job security.

For teachers, this constant flow of new ideologies and methodologies raises questions about what they think and do. And, although every philosophy deserves consideration, and many have merit, none has the *same* value for every teacher and student, or for every school and community.

Despite these ongoing changes, and often without a complete understanding of what a school genuinely offers, parents continue to place their trust in educators.

Thought Starters On Education

For the community, the impact of school education – whether it succeeds or fails – is felt by all of us, as we are swept up in the perpetual cycle of increased spending and costly reform.

I have devoted my working life to my own philosophy of education, and to my genuine desire to improve educational opportunities and outcomes for others.

My work – within education and beyond it – and my wide personal experience have resulted in many projects. Among them, my weekly *Thought Starters* have been written to encourage all of us to extend our views on education outside the circle of our own experiences and to take a vantage point that will give us a wider perspective.

Education affects every government portfolio and every portfolio has an impact on education. Curriculum, funding, business, politics, unions, facilities, world economies, family life, faith and immigration all play a role in the successes or failings of school education.

For any effective lasting reform, we must look beyond the boundaries of schooling, embrace all possibilities and transcend the limitations we currently face.

I hope you will enjoy this first compilation of *Thought Starters*, and do as I love to do most – reflect, respond, share and act.

Chapter 1: Unions

Most public school principals, teachers and employees belong to unions. The implied value of membership is that the legal duties of unions – bargaining for wages and benefits, and providing representation in the event of workplace grievances – are performed fairly for all members. Nothing could be further from the truth.

By its own admission, the Union has a global agenda and has strategically merged its various divisions to this end.

In 1993 the Australian Capital Territory Union (ACTU) began to act on its policy to turn its 300+ unions into 20 or fewer 'super unions'. The Australian Teachers Union (ATU) became the Australian Education Union (AEU), and now anyone connected with 'education' falls under its membership umbrella.

• • •

Thought Starters On Education

💬 A Funding Discussion: Pencil It In!

According to the latest Australian Education Union (AEU) *State of Our Schools* research report (2017), Australian teachers have invested $71 million in pencils and other essential items for students. Think about that for a minute.

The Victorian branch of the AEU has a weekly income of approximately $500,000. This year alone, via the Gonski 2.0 formula, Australian schools have received $17.5 billion in federal government funding. And schools can't afford pencils!

The Australian government has invested a minimum of $10,953 per primary school student and $13,764 per secondary student. And schools can't afford pencils!

A further $104 billion was invested in 600,000 registered not-for-profit organisations in 2014. 36% of these organisations serve education. And schools can't afford pencils!

In 2018-19, $353 million is to be invested in the construction of 12 new schools in Victoria. And schools can't afford pencils!

The Victorian branch of the AEU has a weekly income of approximately $500,000. And schools can't afford pencils!

Despite these massive investments in schools and support services, including not-for profit organisations and unions,

Chapter 1: Unions

schools cannot provide essential items for students. And teachers are expected to cover the cost.

If this isn't a discussion that's worth having with your school principal or local member, then what is?

Better make a note of it right now. But then again, you might not be able to afford a pencil!

First published 30 October 2018

Thought Starters On Education

Playing the Trump Card: Uniting for Merit

Most public school principals, teachers and employees belong to unions. The implied value of membership is that the legal duties of unions – bargaining for wages and benefits, and providing representation in the event of workplace grievances – are performed fairly for all members. Nothing could be further from the truth.

Unions enjoy exclusive and collective bargaining rights. The natural right of principals and teachers to negotiate terms and conditions of their own employment independently is impossible to exercise within this framework of legal exclusivity. For unions, fairness means 'sameness'; currently, merit has no place in public schools.

Unions also owe a duty to the Labor Party – the political party they established. They fund campaigns for State and Federal Labor candidates – an investment that comes from membership fees. Public school principals and teachers who pay union fees also invest in the Labor Party. Those who are not affiliated with the Party cannot re-allocate their investment funds to an alternative political party of their choosing. Currently, political freedom of association does not exist in public schools.

Unions engage with a host of political organisations, programs and campaigns, such as GetUp, Safe Schools and

Chapter 1: Unions

I Give A Gonski. Advertising and advocacy are funded through membership fees, even though many principals and teachers do not support them. There is no freedom to invest union fees in alternative campaigns. Currently, campaign choice does not exist in public schools.

Public schools boast about embracing innovation and creativity. However, exclusive union representation guarantees a non-competitive economic system, which stifles innovation and creativity. Unions shun competition, thwart change and monopolise control over those who are learning and teaching. Currently, liberty does not exist in public schools.

Individual public school principals and teachers have the right to forego union membership, but must abide by the collective wages and conditions negotiated by a union that is affiliated with the Labor Party. Currently, individual 'enterprise' bargaining does not exist in public schools.

Could it be that public schools in Australia are nothing more than tools, used by the union movement and the Labor Party, to chisel out a politically driven socialist manifesto?

On the other hand, perhaps Australia's public schools hold the trump card for innovation, creativity, competition and change. Playing that card might be as simple as introducing collective bargaining to achieve a new definition of fairness – based on merit not 'sameness'.

First Published 16 October 2018

Thought Starters On Education

Schools: Who Needs Them?

'My children don't attend primary school', you might say, 'so primary schools don't really matter that much to me'. You could be right. But think about this.

Spend per child

Does it really matter that, in 2019, primary schools will receive a minimum of $10,576 for each student enrolled? When calculating the figure for the average class size of 24 students, that's $253,824 per classroom annually – or $6,345 weekly – from the taxpayers' budget.

Does it really matter that taxpayers fork out $254,824 for the average primary classroom of 24 students, regardless of location, demographic, year level, teacher performance, student outcome or the school leaders that determine how the budget is spent?

Perhaps it doesn't matter at all, and you could be forgiven for thinking so. That's because, according to the International Labor Organisation (ILO) – an agency of the United Nations – the education sector isn't considered an essential service. There is no need to measure return on investment, because it doesn't matter how much or how little we spend: education services aren't essential. They don't really matter.

Chapter 1: Unions

Cleaning - an essential service

But here's the catch. The cleaning of schools does matter. The cleaning of schools is an essential service.

After a survey conducted by the trade union group United Voice, the Department of Education Victoria introduced ministerial orders, commencing July 2018, with regard to the maintenance of a Contract Cleaners Panel for government approved cleaning contractors for schools.

Principals must now be held responsible for cleaners they no longer have the authority to hire.

Instead, they must rely on one of 8 mega cleaning services authorised by the Department of Education. What might this mean for you?

School closures

What if one, or all, of the 8 mega cleaning services contracted to clean Victorian schools were to go on strike? Could school cleaning become a health and safety issue and force schools to close? And if negotiations took days, weeks, or even months, who would look after the children? What impact would this have on families, employers and workplaces, including other essential services? If other States and Territories followed Victoria's new model, would primary schools matter to you then?

Thought Starters On Education

Could it be that in Victoria schools are no longer places of learning, but potential means of social control of the highest order?

If you think primary schools have little to do with you unless your children attend one, perhaps you should think again!

First Published 6 August 6 2018

Chapter 1: Unions

Strike One, You're Out! The Unions: A Blight on Public Education

Less than four weeks into the 2018 school year and Australian public school teachers prepared to strike over an apparently crushing workload.

The new Enterprise Agreement, sought by the Australian Education Union (Victorian Branch), is driven by negotiations perceived to be in the best interests of staff and students. The draft agreement, if successful would affect every Victorian.

Public schools are the heartbeat of local communities. The success, or otherwise, of any public school has long-term and often lifelong implications that span generations. Schools are also big business – the business of teaching – and that business belongs to the people of Victoria, not just to those employed in public schools today.

As reported in the *Age* on 11 February 2018, the union has advised the general public that they are seeking the following improvements to the teaching profession:

- More time to plan and assess students
- Employ 2000 more teachers
- A 21% pay rise over 3 years

Thought Starters On Education

- Protected industrial action
- A maximum of 20 students per classroom (K-12)
- A reduction of non-permanent teachers

What wasn't reported were the many clauses in the proposed new Enterprise Agreement that will have ramifications for the teaching profession – in Victoria and the nation.

Some of these include:

- School councils to be employers – with union representation on council
- Union and employer working parties to be established in all schools
- Teachers represented by the AEU and all other unions under s201 (2), as noted by the Fair Work Commission
- EAL (English language learner) classes not to exceed twelve students
- Personal leave to be increased to 15 days per year which would be cumulative
- Where personal leave has been used, additional personal leave to be granted
- Teachers who are deemed to be in a poor state of health would be entitled to remain on personal leave
- 3 months infectious disease leave
- 5 days bereavement leave

Chapter 1: Unions

- War service leave to be increased to 100 days
- Principals to retain their position and pay, while holding a full-time position elsewhere
- Increased union representation in schools, with 2 hours per week allocated for industrial matters – to be deducted from face-to-face teaching time
- Union representatives to be granted 2 days per term to attend union meetings with the *Department of Education* to cover costs for replacement teachers.
- 5 days leave to attend trade union training courses
- Domestic Violence leave (to be advised)
- Employees can request changes to flexible work practices, including for IVF treatment, parenting responsibilities, and if they are over 55

Nowhere in the proposed Enterprise Agreement does the union nominate the need for further training, personal development or upskilling on a regular basis, the removal of compulsory government programs, or the review of the Victorian Curriculum.

Neither does it provide solace to the thousands of dedicated teachers and principals who already work under difficult conditions, due to the failure of the union to remove ineffective teachers, principals, or practices.

Thought Starters On Education

Union survey

Survey results involving less than 28% of the AEU's membership were used to compile a case for negotiating with the Victorian Government; the Enterprise Agreement, not surprisingly, is yet to be finalised. Might this suggest that there is a small contingent of AEU members driving this agenda, while the majority is disengaged – even embarrassed – about the union's threats?

Enterprise Agreements are generally of interest only to those employed in the sector in question; this one is an exception.

No-one is immune from the implications of the AEU's agenda.

Here's a snapshot of what the AEU survey claims:

- Teachers are overworked. 80% of teachers work unpaid overtime every week.
- Teachers work an average 53 hours per week
- 80% of teachers work 15 hours of unpaid overtime every week.

While these statistics appear alarming, what is more alarming is the implication that teachers spend more time on duties other than teaching. What is the basis of these claims? The current teaching workload (38 hours per week) involves teachers in face-to-face teaching for less than 50% of that time (about 22 hours). Does the union know

Chapter 1: Unions

how the other 16 hours per week are being spent? Furthermore, the previous EBA negotiated by the AEU, includes time for non-teaching responsibilities.

How has the role of teacher changed?

Over two-thirds of teachers say they don't have time to plan their classes.

Effective teaching requires less long-term planning and more short term observation, leading to immediate action – teaching, prompting and reinforcing of strategies, behaviours, skills and understandings. Effective teachers manage their time and their capabilities with confidence.

Does the union allege that almost one-third of Prep to Year 12 public school teachers – 38,000 fully qualified professionals – cannot teach?

Schools cannot be measured by the traditional 8-hour day. They are currently only required to be open for business for 40 weeks of the year – that is, when students are in attendance. Students have 12 weeks of vacation time per year and teachers 4. This gives teachers 40 weeks of teaching time, plus 8 weeks or 304 hours across the year to work flexibly to perform other duties.

Many principals choose to work longer hours during the school term to take advantage of the flexible work options currently offered. If the alleged 60 hours per week worked during term time were spread across the calendar year,

Thought Starters On Education

which includes the 8 weeks of flexible work arrangements available, principals would actually work the same number of hours as teachers do.

Almost half of principals' time is spent on administration and compliance

Principals work toward their leadership positions. Their applications must include evidence that they can manage a combination of educational and administrative duties – including delegation. Before accepting the role, they are acutely aware of the responsibilities that go with it. Principals represent the government as the employer of teachers. Does the union allege that more than 1500 schools and 590,000 students attend facilities where the Principals' administration and compliance responsibilities determine the strength or otherwise of the face-to-face teaching of teachers? The AEU (Victorian Branch) represents both principals and teachers – or does it?

Here's what the union says teachers and principals are seeking:

- 85% of teachers need more time within school hours for planning and assessing student learning.
- 88.6% of principals want an increased budget.
- 88.8% of principals want to reduce compliance requirements.
- 86.1% of principals want more specialist staff for wellbeing work.

Chapter 1: Unions

- 81.5% of principals want more administrative support.
- 77.6% of principals want an increased capacity to attract and retain effective teachers.
- 70.8% of principals want more teacher aides.

These potential solutions highlight a collective frustration in schools and the need for government, school councils, and the parent community to have a complete understanding of the underlying issues that exist in our public places of learning.

That 77.6% of principals want greater autonomy over staff (Point 6) is of serious concern. Does this suggest that over 1200 public schools in Victoria have a mixture of effective and ineffective teachers? Does the AEU allege that principals and teachers have not requested external assistance, professional and personal development, or more effective measures to transition between schools, or indeed across vocations?

Why is this so important?

It can't be said too often: Our public schools are the heartbeat of the community.

Given the dire situation the union presents, one must wonder whether teachers must take drastic actions of their own and place their own children in independent or catholic schools.

Thought Starters On Education

Threats of strike action are based on fear and scaremongering. Victorians are better than that.

So the best thing that could happen would be for this strike to go ahead. Teachers and principals will lose their pay; students will be without a place to go; and parents will have to make urgent alternative arrangements. The greater the impact, the greater the opportunity for us all to become actively involved.

Strike action will be an opportunity for us to take a position – one from which we can stand up to these dangerous rorts.

We also have a responsibility to be fully informed. We must ask questions; every Victorian must understand where the problems lie, what the suggested solutions are, and to what extent they apply to every local school.

We must participate confidently to raise the level of dialogue about where we want our children to attend school. This will encourage parents and communities to examine all possible choices, rather than remain trapped in a union driven, one-size-fits-all system, which is failing.

This is a call to action

- Find out who is your union representative at your local school.
- Ask for a community forum and, if your request is not granted, start one of your own.

Chapter 1: Unions

- Write to your local member of parliament seeking support
- Contact your local newspaper and rally support
- Do your homework. Visit the AEU website.

Our teachers and principals deserve better; our parents and children deserve better; and our communities deserve better.

Let's work together to choose a world-leading public education system that will help our State and nation prosper.

The AEU has a membership of 48,000 workers. This includes teachers, principals, support staff, early childhood, TAFE and adult education workers. It also includes day services, employment officers, program managers and CEO's in the disability sector.

First Published 16 February 2018

Thought Starters On Education

Propaganda, Infiltration, Legislation: Why Unions Should Stay Out of Classrooms

'America is like a healthy body and its resistance is threefold: its patriotism, its morality, and its spiritual life. If we can undermine these three areas, America will collapse from within' —Joseph Stalin

So what does a Russian leader's observation on the U.S. have to do with Australia? Everything!

Our young nation, once full of promise, is collapsing under the weight of public naivety, cleverly disguised as fairness and equality. And it's happening, courtesy of Victoria – the Machiavellian State that claims to be the Education State – and its preferred place of national infiltration, the classroom.

Although the unions and the Labor Party of today aren't what they were twenty, fifty or one hundred years ago, it is accurate to say that Socialists, Trade Unions and the Fabian Society can be credited for the creation of the Labor Party. The questions to ask are these: Just who is who in the Labor Party? How many factions exist right now? How much power does the union wield?

Some might say our classrooms have become breeding places for factional unrest under the guise of union care and concern.

Chapter 1: Unions

Three more questions come to mind: What do teachers really know and understand about those who purport to represent teachers' best interests? Is the infiltration of the classroom, by unions, a deliberate tactic to further their cause: the creation of a national working class? Do our politicians understand that the unions are the masters and they, the politicians, are the servants?

Five reasons why unions are a blight on Australian classrooms

1. BIASED POLITICAL ALLIANCE

As co-creators of the Labor movement, the unions have strategically infiltrated the nation's workplaces – including the classrooms. During the late 1970s, for example, the Australian Council of Salaried and Professional Associations (ACSPA) and the Council of Australian Government Employee Associations (CAGEO) – the representatives of non-manual workers including banking, insurance, teaching, local government and nursing – merged with the Australian Council of Trade Unions. Can a body genuinely represent workers and align itself with a political party at the same time? Is this a clear and direct conflict of interest?

2. STRATEGIC CULTURAL CONTROL

It is understood that unions provide a formal mechanism for collective representation. But what does collective representation mean?

Thought Starters On Education

- In 1848 the Anti-transportation League was established to lobby against penal transportation to Australia
- In 1879 the Inter-Colonial Trade Union Congress (ICTUC) – the forerunner to the ACTU – opposed Chinese immigration
- In 1898 the ICTUC extended its immigration restrictions – from the Chinese to all non-European peoples.

Today, unions love to include the non-English in their collective representation. Using the classroom as a vehicle for access, they campaign for funding using a model that provides loadings for children of non-English speaking backgrounds.

3. STRATEGIC SOCIAL CONTROL

In 1993 the Australian Teachers Union (ATU) became the Australian Education Union (AEU). By its own admission, the Union has a global agenda and has strategically merged its various divisions to this end. Not surprisingly, also in 1993, the ACTU began to act on its policy to turn its 300+ unions into 20 or fewer 'super unions', bringing anyone connected with 'education' under the membership umbrella.

Further questions:

- Have the unions had a hand in the promotion of terms used in classrooms such as, 'life-long learning' so that super unions have broader reach and control?

Chapter 1: Unions

- Does the existence of super unions mean the term 'Education State' can be used to establish a union-controlled 'Education Nation?'
- Is it possible that Building the Education Revolution (BER) and Digital Education Revolution (DER) – bribery in classrooms – were tactical steps in that direction?

4. STRATEGIC INTERNATIONAL ALLIANCE

In that same pivotal year of 1993, Education International (EI) – a global education union – was also formed. Some of its principal aims are to promote unity among all independent and democratic trade unions within the educational sector, and united action and cooperation with independent trade unions in other sectors, and thereby contribute to the further development of the international trade union movement.

What does unity really mean? Are we keeping abreast of State and Federal legislation? Is it possible that terms including, '21st Century Skills', 'Anywhere Anytime Learning', 'Global Education' and 'Global Citizenship', are subtly promoting the idea our children become employees of a worldwide trade union working class network, while they are still in the classroom?

5. STRATEGIC GENDER POLITICS

The union acknowledges its alliance to various causes. One of them is the Women's Rights at Work campaign, which aims for social change to achieve gender equity.

Thought Starters On Education

However, gender equity is the process of achieving fairness for women and men and the union does not support a campaign for Men's Rights at Work.

The union also supports the *Safe Schools Program* and the *Safe Schools Coalition*, an initiative established under the previous Labor government. Disguised as an anti-bullying program, it could be said the *Safe Schools Program* is really a vehicle for cry-bullies to gain collective classroom representation on a national scale via gender-based propaganda.

While the Victorian State government works diligently to infiltrate classrooms, the Federal opposition, currently led by a professional unionist, might be deceptively doing the same, with its brand, 'Your Child, Our Future.' Its stated objective is, 'more individual attention for students, better trained teachers, (for) every school, every child. Government, Independent or Catholic.' Is this the propaganda of diligent socialists, edging towards national accumulated growth and one global government? How? With a slow creep toward ownership of State schools, now owned by the people, and of Independent schools, now owned by the church or other independent establishments.

Classrooms are places of learning and teaching. They also occupy very valuable parcels of land across the country. It's often said that the way to control people is to control land. Is this more cunning and duplicity from the union? Is it really aiming for control via the nation's classrooms?

First Published 24 October 2017

Chapter 2: Gender and Sexuality

Sexuality and gender education happens in schools. It might be in the intended curriculum – via an open and transparent agreed-upon set of content and standards. It might be in the hidden curriculum – with opinions, values, attitudes, and approaches that might or might not be in sync with your own.

There is also a growing number of educational and political leaders throughout the world, who feel that schools are the most appropriate places to equip children and youth with the knowledge and skills required to identify their gender and become sexually active and healthy individuals.

Wherever you live, and however the programs are packaged, sexuality and gender education definitely happens in schools.

• • •

Thought Starters On Education

Watch Out for Women

Between May and July 2017, one in five teachers considered leaving the profession. Why? Because of continuing high levels of on the job stress, and problems associated with work-life balance. And almost half of the teachers surveyed said they felt stressed "most of the time" or "fairly often" during a typical week.

Australia's teaching profession is predominantly female. About 75% of secondary teachers and 82% of primary school teachers are women. In 2016, there were approximately 310,000 full-time female teachers.

Our Watch, funded by the Federal Government, was established to 'end violence against women and their children'. It's also the organisation responsible for the *'Respectful Relationships Education in Schools'* program for Australian schools.

Our Watch claims:

- One in three Australian women has experienced physical violence, since the age of 15.
- One in five Australian women has experienced sexual violence.

Chapter 2: Gender and Sexuality

If the claims are true, in Australian schools:

- up to 100,000 full-time female teachers who have experienced violence are teaching our children about 'respectful relationships'
- up to 62,000 full-time female teachers who have experienced sexual violence are teaching our children about 'respectful relationships'
- up to 100,000 female teachers who have considered leaving the profession due to stress are teaching our children 'Stress Management' – Unit 5 of the Respectful Relationships program.

If you think there's a problem here, you're right. To make matters worse, the Australian Education Union claims nearly every teacher has endured workplace bullying.

I'll say it again. Australia's teaching profession is made up predominantly of women.

Therefore, some women who are allegedly qualified to teach our children how to be respectful and safe are abusing other women in the workplace.

Of its own admission, *Our Watch* states that gender-based violence is, 'violence that is specifically directed against a woman because she is a woman, or that affects women disproportionately'.

Thought Starters On Education

Could it be said that *Our Watch* has no place in Australian schools? Or should it be said that the use of the word 'violence' is merely a tactic to secure ridiculous amounts of funding for scare campaigns designed to disguise the real and genuine issues of 'bullying' that women face, at the hands of their own gender?

This may well be the beginning of a confronting but necessary national outcry. For the sake of our women and children – let's hope so.

First Published August 30 2017

Chapter 2: Gender and Sexuality

The Weight of Trust: Sex, School and Society

Sexuality education happens in schools. It might be in the intended curriculum – via an open and transparent agreed-upon set of content and standards. It might be in the hidden curriculum, with its opinions, values, attitudes, and approaches that might or might not be in sync with your own. Either way, it definitely happens.

According to the United Nations Economic, Scientific and Cultural Organisation (UNESCO), "The primary goal of sexuality education is that children and young people become equipped with the knowledge, skills, and values to make responsible choices about their sexual and social relationships…"

But what is the most appropriate way to make sure children and young people are "equipped"? Who should do it, and where?

What's happening around the world?

Pro-choice research from the United States suggests 80% of Americans support a blended curriculum that emphasises the benefits of abstinence, while also including practical lessons about condom and contraceptive use. In response, President Obama removed funding for Abstinence Only Until Marriage (AOUM) programs in his final budget, and has instead proposed increased funding for comprehensive sex education in schools.

The United Kingdom

In the UK, Personal, Social, Health and Economic education (PSHE), which includes sex education, is considered to play a crucial part in preparing young people for life. However, in early 2016, then Prime Minister David Cameron rejected attempts to mandate sex education in all British schools, a move that led female parliamentarians to hold up the gender card in dispute.

Canada

A pilot project in Quebec, Canada has seen 19 schools delivering sexuality education for students from K-12. If successful, the intention is to introduce a 'no exemptions' sexuality education curriculum across the province in 2017. However, delays in the pilot have raised concerns over teacher capacity and reluctance to teach sensitive content. Other teachers have taken matters into their own hands, delivering a hidden curriculum on explicit sexuality education of their choosing. If the mandatory curriculum goes ahead, parents will be refused the option of withdrawing their children from classes while sexuality content is being taught.

Sweden has a long established history of sexuality education. However, despite a compulsory program, introduced in 1956, the inconsistencies in teacher qualifications, and

Chapter 2: Gender and Sexuality

time allocation are preventing effective implementation. Some teachers dedicate only one day, while others allocate a six-week block to sexuality education.

New Zealand

New Zealand has taken a collaborative and respectful approach. It is compulsory for sexuality education to be taught in schools, until the end of Year 10, but parents have the right to withdraw their children from these classes. School Boards are also mandated to consult with their community every two years about their Sexuality Education Policy and curriculum content. This allows parents to make an informed choice for their child.

Singapore

In Singapore sexuality education is included as part of Character and Citizenship Education, and there is an opt-out clause for parents.

Australia is more like Quebec, where states or provinces have their own *guardians* or drivers of curriculum. Despite delays to the Quebec pilot, and parental uproar, complete with placards protesting 'Math not Masturbation. Science not Sex', Victoria is poised to mandate sexuality education in 2017.

For centuries, philosophers have studied and written about learning and teaching. In about 380BC, Plato wrote *The Republic,* a dialogue that included his thoughts on the ideal society and the education of children. In his writing, he rejects the family unit in favour of *'guardians'*.

He reasoned that it would avoid nepotism and the amassing of private wealth. More importantly, he argued that children were the responsibility of the State, and no parent should know his own child, nor any child his parents.

It seems that throughout the world we have educational and political leaders who feel that schools are the most appropriate places to equip children and youth with the knowledge and skills required to be sexually active and healthy individuals.

On the other hand, there are leaders who, like me, believe that transparency and choice create respectful relationships and a healthy school environment. They want to build communities that demonstrate co-operation, and equip families to make healthy choices for their own lives and the lives of others.

What all educational leaders and parents should be asking

10 ESSENTIAL QUESTIONS

1. What is being taught in sexuality education classes?
2. To what extent are the rights of parents being relinquished?

Chapter 2: Gender and Sexuality

3. To what extent are the responsibilities and personal beliefs of teachers being compromised?
4. How will teachers become qualified to manage sensitive content effectively?
5. How will my school manage the implications of the hidden curriculum on sex education?
6. How will my school ensure the views of parents are respected, regardless of nationality, religion or family background?
7. Is our school prepared to take full responsibility for sexuality education?
8. What is already being taught via the hidden curriculum? How well do we know our staff?
9. How will we measure the value of sexuality education?
10. Do my personal values, beliefs, and attitudes match those of our school?

All schools have their share of dedicated professionals, complacent individuals, and politically driven antagonists. The curriculum, including Sexuality Education, is open to interpretation, and it does not deliver itself. Its success or otherwise is the result of human interaction and human values.

Whether your school already has an intended sexuality education curriculum – mandated or otherwise – or plans to introduce one, your greatest challenge will continue to be the hidden curriculum.

Sexuality education is already happening in schools, but not always where, and how we think.

First Published 2 November 2016

Chapter 2: Gender and Sexuality

Is the Male Teacher an Endangered Species?

Country	%	Country	%	Country	%
Austria	91.6	Belgium	81.8	New Zealand	83.8
Canada	74.4	Chile	81.3	Poland	85.4
Czech Republic	94	Estonia	91.1	Australia	81.7
Finland	79.8	France	82.1	USA	87.1
Germany	86.8	Greece	70	India	49.5
Hungary	96.8	Iceland	81.9	Indonesia	61.5
Iceland	81.9	Ireland	87	Norway	75
Israel	85.3	Italy	95.9	Portugal	80.1
Japan	64.8	Korea	78.4	Slovenia	97.2
Latvia	92.8	Luxemburg	75.8	China	62.6
Mexico	67.7	Netherlands	86.2	Saudi Arabia	52

Where have all the male teachers gone? The table above shows the percentage of female teachers in primary/elementary schools around the world, in 2015.

Do you agree that these statistics are unacceptable? Who, or what, is driving this trend? What is the philosophy or agenda behind it? What would be the consequences if it were to continue? Do you want a world in which men become extinct in our schools?

The world needs men. Schools need men. The world needs to value men.

This isn't about playing another gender card. It's the beginning of a humane and critical movement – for everyone's sake.

Thought Starters On Education

We must engage in robust debate and listen to wide-ranging views – especially those with which we don't immediately agree.

We must explore all possibilities, regardless of their complexity, if we are to achieve necessary fundamental change: to raise the bar of education in schools and bring more men back into our classrooms.

Would you agree that these statistics are unacceptable? Should you do something about it? Have you the courage to do it? I certainly have the courage. I've started a movement for change. Help me continue it.

First Published 3 April 2018

Chapter 2: Gender and Sexuality

Remaining Abreast of Equality

The concept of quality is a fascinating one. Although many inequalities have been rectified over time – and rightly so – the truth is, absolute equality will never be possible. It might even be true to say that the more strenuously people seek equality, the more divided society becomes.

Earlier this year Australian Senator Larissa Waters stepped on to the world stage by breastfeeding while in Parliament. Women's rights advocates were ecstatic. But why? The Senator merely proved that, for some women, status affords them rights that others do not have. In this instance, she effectively spat on the sisterhood of all women – particularly those in the public service.

Had the Senator been advocating for Family Violence Laws to include an age limit at which women can breastfeed, her actions might have been more widely accepted.

Currently, there are approximately 320,000 full-time female teachers in Australia. Have you ever seen a female teacher breastfeed while teaching a class or performing other responsibilities such as yard duty?

As you enter Australia after an international flight, have you ever encountered a female customs officer breastfeeding as she examines your luggage?

Thought Starters On Education

Have you ever encountered a female police officer breastfeeding on traffic duty, or while operating a booze bus?

Equality is the state of being equal – especially in status, rights and opportunities.

A particular time and set of circumstances made it possible for the Senator to breastfeed –something that is not possible for all women to do in conditions under which they work. She was able to breastfeed because of status and parliamentary privilege. Quite simply, she did it because she could.

The majority of Australian women live according to their standards of morality, justice and honourable conduct.

Could it be said that the women's rights agenda, purporting to stand up for all women, is merely a tactic to disguise the real and genuine issue: the pursuit of power by hypocritical, elitist, self-serving individuals? If so, it undermines the right of women to be themselves – reasonable and self-determining.

This might be the start of a confronting, but necessary national outcry on the distinction between equality for self and quality for all. For the sake of real women – let's hope so.

First Published 19 September 2017

Chapter 3: Funding and School Choice

Public schools currently receive 20% of funding from the Commonwealth Government and 80% from State and Territory Governments. On the other hand, private schools currently receive 80% of funding from the Commonwealth Government and 20% from State and Territory Governments.

School funding, therefore, is equitable. The way in which schools invest their funding, however, is rarely ever the same, if at all.

If schools were no longer funded directly, but instead, financial contributions were made directly to families, what might education in Australia look like?

● ● ●

Thought Starters On Education

You Oughta Be Congratulated

What would you do with a redeemable voucher of, let's say, $11,000 per year, to be used for your child's education? Would you stay with the school your child currently attends? Or would you 'shop around' to find a more suitable fit for you and your child? Would you spend more than the value of the voucher, from your own budget, in the belief that more money means greater opportunity for your child?

Whatever your choice, you would think more carefully about where and how that money was spent. You'd monitor everything more closely: what your child was being taught; the teaching staff; the extra-curricular opportunities; and other investments made by the school. You'd want to be sure your investment was being spent wisely. Above all, you would advocate for your child. Wouldn't you?

Well, here's the good news. You are given a lump sum toward your child's education every year, and it's called school funding. It bypasses you and is paid, by the taxpayer, directly to the school of your choosing.

If you have done the right thing by your child, and you've chosen to live in a regional area, or you've chosen to live on a low income, or you are an immigrant, indigenous or bi-lingual family then you're in for a bonus. That's right, extra money will be paid directly to the school, because of your life choices and because those choices directly affect your child's performance at school.

Chapter 3: Funding and School Choice

However, if you have failed your child, and you have worked hard and studied hard, you are well educated, well paid, and speak fluent English, and have chosen to live in the CBD or outer lying suburbs, then your life choices create a disadvantage for your child. There is no bonus attached to any of your choices.

Regardless of where you were born, where you live, how much you earn, or what language you speak, if your child is gifted, passionate about learning or, on the other hand, has been failed by poor school performance, then… bad luck. There's little you can do but accept your place at the back of the queue. There's no more money for you.

What would you do with a redeemable voucher of, let's say $11,000 per year, to be used for your child's education?

Wouldn't you demand value for money, greater choice, and a louder voice for you and your child? Chances are there'd be competition for your investment, and chances are the value, choice and voice you demand might not come only in the form of schooling as we know it. Wouldn't that be a bonus?

First Published 1 May 2018

Thought Starters On Education

Exchanging Printed Paper for Effective Education Services: A Wise Choice?

'Backwards by default' is the most appropriate way to describe the Senate's decision, on 23rd June 2017, to pass the Gonski 2.0 $23.5 billion funding model for Australian schools. It's the extreme height of political pragmatism with regard to the most important public policy in the nation. The lure of money wins again. And, as expected, there's already activity buzzing around what many believe is the next most important question: how shall we spend it?

No surprises here. Any amount of much-needed profound and honest reflection might be too much. Can we handle the truth? Especially if it forces many of us – parents, teachers, principals, lawyers, politicians, and bureaucrats – to admit that we might have failed so many children, including our own, by accepting the state of education in Australia – and for far too long.

Is this a choice we have willingly made, or is lack of choice at the centre of increasingly poor school performance?

Result = Responsibility NOT Response + Ability

It is true that commencing in 2019, primary schools can look forward to a minimum of $10,576 per student and $13,290 for secondary schools; the schools, however, not

Chapter 3: Funding and School Choice

schooling itself, will take the winner's seat. Parents and children stand to receive nothing more than what they already have. For the sake of a quick result, Australians have been dealt a reactive blow – another 'piggy bank and tuck shop' solution.

Surely common sense would have included asking the difficult questions, accepting the reality of the findings and, more importantly, creating a nationally inclusive, differentiated model for education, with compassion firmly at the heart of every responsible action. It's no longer acceptable to aspire to world leading opportunities, without facing the challenges associated with achieving them. We all have to toughen up and take responsibility.

If there were wider choices, would we be encouraged to take greater responsibility?

Faith or funding

The Commonwealth, States and Territories' main stumbling block over funding for schooling is based on faith, but religion, or life view, lies at the heart of education – it is about responsible citizenship. The naïve notion that public schools are secular suggests – or accepts – that culture and citizenship do not exist. Regardless of the faith or life view that informs it, every school has a culture. The question is this: if the culture is *not* based on a specific faith or life view, then what is its base? What is the difference between a school culture and the culture of schooling? It would seem that printed paper offers the answer. Money not choice!

Could it be said that parents, forced to find the necessary funds to enrol their children in faith-based schools, are being penalised for choosing faith as the foundation for their children's education? Could it also be said that these parents are being penalised because the State provides public schooling, and that anything resembling a faith-based school is seen as an entitlement rather than a personal investment in their children's education?

If faith were replaced with 'Australian Culture', how would funding look? What would parental contributions and not-for-profit support look like?

Vague intention or reality

Behind every policy is a person. Gonski 2.0 was constructed using a sampling of NAPLAN data, postcodes, and loadings for disability, languages other than English, socio-economic status, and location. It demonstrates a plan of action that aims to achieve a business objective; it shows little or no compassion for the individuals in question – the 'persons' behind this policy.

Consider these points:

- The formula's target labelling – for instance 'disabled student'. Behind the formula is a parent in need of assistance to educate a child, who is managing a disability.

Chapter 3: Funding and School Choice

- Low-income families in commission and rental housing share postcodes with affluent families. Postcode does not equate to taxable income; taxable income, however, more accurately reflects educational affordability.

- Adults of low socio-economic standing do not necessarily demonstrate ineptitude or illiteracy, just as affluent families are not necessarily free of disability, language barriers or academic challenges.

- The highest NAPLAN results for schools are not necessarily equivalent to the students' best performances.

Schools are unique, as a family demographic is. The Gonski 2.0 inclusion of a 'capacity to pay' formula assumes that fee paying parents exist only in the private and denominational sectors. Capacity to pay does not include families of children attending public schools – leaving the use of demographics and postcodes across the board questionable.

If the funding model is based on inaccuracies, what then is the expected return on investment?

Registration or provision

With regard to funding, the emphasis has been placed on public, private and denominational schools. Little has been said about home schooling. Approximately 30,000 Australian families choose to home-school their children or to access distance education.

Thought Starters On Education

Families that choose to home-school must register with the State or Territory in which they reside, but according to legislation – the Education and Training Reform Act 2006 of Victoria, for instance – schools are considered to be places in which education takes place during normal school hours, with the exception of home schooling. This shows the distinction between an investment in schools and an investment in schooling or education. However, section 1.2.1(d) of that same Act states: 'Parents have the right to choose an appropriate education for their child'.

Is the home schooling issue the only evidence that investment in schools is not an investment in schooling or education?

Systemic contradictions: funding or managing

The Commonwealth Government will provide 20% of its funding for public schools, and 80% will go toward private schools. State and Territory Governments are expected to pay the larger portion of 80% for public schools and the remaining 20% for private schools. However equitable, government funding – regardless of its origin – does not equate to equitable provision or management of schooling.

To reference the State Government of Victorian Education once more, its website states, 'Victorian legislation clearly states that instruction in the standard curriculum program must be provided free of charge to all students in Victorian government schools. However, free instruction refers to teaching staff, administration and the provision of facilities

Chapter 3: Funding and School Choice

in connection with instruction of the standard curriculum program. In other words, government funding is essentially paying for wages, buildings and grounds. The website also states that, 'schools decide on the learning program they offer, based on the needs and aspirations of the school community'. Parents are asked to meet costs that are beyond the 'standard curriculum', and no two school communities or public schools are necessarily the same.

Everything considered then, Victorian schools are no different from denominational or private schools. The same is true in other States and Territories that offer select entry schools, gender exclusive schools, and schools that offer the International Baccalaureate.

If the community can choose the learning program, and if funding is linked to students, why is the funding given to schools?

Resourcing or review

Gonksi 2.0 promises the establishment of a National School Resourcing Board to review the distribution of funds to schools. Providing checks and balances with regard to funding is clearly an incentive in this model. Money is a resource. A more intelligent way to use this money would be investing it in schooling. A review of ways to reduce acceptable waste in schools, as well as ways to replicate wise investment must also include a review of the standard curriculum, and the individuals that deliver it.

Thought Starters On Education

Can teachers be up-skilled, transferred or transitioned out of schools in the same way as a school's buildings and grounds can be remodelled, renovated or closed?

Choice or control

In 2016, the Australian Bureau of Statistics showed that in Australian schools there were more than 3.5 million full-time students, and almost 0.5 million teachers. Funding for schools includes the provision of wages for teachers. As employees, teachers are free to apply for positions in a range of schools, and to find an environment that suits their professional needs. As in all other professions, they have the opportunity to apply for promotions and positions of leadership outside the classroom, and to apply for leave, or changes to working hours, including part-time options. Regardless of their choices, they will be paid.

Students, on the other hand, are subjected to compulsory school attendance. For them, there is nothing that equates to the flexible school hours, promotion, or flexible leave arrangements that teachers have. Furthermore, any schooling that takes place in schools before 8.45am or after 3.45pm – known as 'before and after school care' – comes at a cost to parents. It would seem that Gonski 2.0 is a funding source based on a cookie cutter philosophy that views a school as a business that operates from 8.45am to 3.45pm, rather than as one possible source of schooling?

Are schools designed to employ rather than to educate?

Chapter 3: Funding and School Choice

Contribution or consumption

At the Commonwealth level, schools are funded predominantly from the acquisition of income tax, GST and capital gains tax. At the State level, schools funding comes predominantly from stamp duty and land tax.

Parental contributions are expected in every school, regardless of location, denomination or sector. Just as the Catholic sector distributes funds between dioceses to support lower income families and communities, higher income earners, property investors, independently wealthy taxpayers, and businesses contribute to Australian schools at large – regardless of the number of children they have.

Families that choose to send their children to denominational or private schools, not only pay private school fees, after tax, they also contribute to schools across the nation through their payment of taxes.

If tax payers know the cost of Medicare, private health insurance, rates and land tax, and can choose to invest accordingly, should they also be able to choose whether or not they invest in schools or schooling, and to what value?

Area or academia

Increased opportunity for students to further their education to Year 12 and beyond has brought resounding success for many. For others, however, it has come at a grave cost.

Thought Starters On Education

During the 1930s, Tasmania, like other Australian States and Territories, struggled with the cost of maintaining rural schools, and with the limited opportunities, they provided for students. To counter the problem, the State introduced 'area schools'. They offered a curriculum rich in citizenship, and specialised in practical subjects directly related to the character of the local districts. To ensure students weren't limited to a life on a farm, these schools eventually became obsolete. They were, however, attempting to provide schooling for the much-needed workforce beyond the 'white collar' middle class.

There is much to be learned from them:

- First, an over emphasis on technology now tends to limit the use and development of different skill sets and interests. Agriculture, culinary skills, sport, the arts, music and manufacturing remain essential elements of a diverse and balanced society. Narrowing opportunity increases the risk of disengagement, abuse, suicide, depression, welfare and unemployment, to name a few.

- Second, the current funding model provides loadings for students in rural areas. Let's use a simple equation to consider the waste. Assume every child in Australia is provided a base rate of $1. The loading of $1 applies to rural locations. A rural school has 5 children and a regional school has 100. The regional school receives $100 and the rural school receives $10. Both schools offer the standard curriculum; the regional school,

Chapter 3: Funding and School Choice

however, has greater financial flexibility. The same can be said for the loadings for disability, non-English speaking students, and indigenous students. Spreading the funds across more than 9000 schools limits schools to standard academia, as opposed to giving them the opportunity to specialize in a given area.

What is the cost to the Australian budget and on Australian society, when Gonski 2.0 invests in schools rather than in schooling that would prepare everyone for citizenship and employment, regardless of capacity?

Fundamentals or foundations

If schools are to have any fundamental impact on responsible citizenship, those planning to enter the teaching profession must themselves be the products of quality teacher training.

A 2015 ACER review of *The Teacher Workforce in Australia: Supply, Demand and Data*, has identified 'out-of-field' teachers – those who teach beyond their qualification. It is a grave concern.

Statistics from this report reveal the percentage of teachers teaching out-of-field in the following subjects:

- Mathematics and physics – about 20%
- History – 25%
- Computing/IT – 30%

- Geography – 40%
- English – % unknown

Major factors that lead to out-of-field teaching include:

- 35% (3,300) schools having fewer than 400 students; and the related impact on class size
- the expectation that schools offer a diverse curriculum, regardless of school size or location
- teachers having to cover a range of subjects
- competent teachers being placed with senior students (to boost Year 12 results)
- out-of-field teachers being placed with lower year levels

In addition, primary school teachers – qualified as generalist teachers – are expected to teach any of eight different year levels, across every area of the curriculum – all of which demand increased complexity of knowledge, understanding and skills. Furthermore, teachers aspiring to leadership and principal roles, who would then determine staffing, are expected to apply for, and perform in, such positions without any additional formal qualifications.

In 1964 the Martin Report or *The Report of Tertiary Training in Australia* recommended that an *autonomous* Board of Teacher Education be established in each State, and charged with the authority to advise government in relation to future developments in teaching training. Its view was that the educational experience of any child, gained from

Chapter 3: Funding and School Choice

kindergarten to university, depends largely on the extent to which teachers are prepared to perform their tasks.

A further recommendation was that the Board 'should also become the channel through which Commonwealth funds would be made available for the development of the preparation of teachers'.

Succumbing to the 'I Give a Gonski' philosophy places schools in a lucrative financial position. It places teachers and students, however, in an increasingly vulnerable one – the implications of which include teacher stress and burnout, student disengagement, and increased rates of truancy and suspension.

Gonksi 2.0 is a $23.5 billion funding model for Australian schools. It might well become known, however, as one of Australia's most radical investments in welfare, unless there is a parallel investment in quality teaching.

What are the real reasons for the encouragement of unskilled teachers? And who's behind it?

Need or want

Imagine you were given $10,576 or $13,290 to invest in your child's education. How would you use it? Would you choose a school? What type of school? Might you invest in one that was a better fit for your faith, your child's ability and interests, or in a convenient location? Would you 'top up' the funds you were given, to give you greater choice?

Thought Starters On Education

Whatever your final decision, you'd certainly think more carefully about where and how any investment were spent. If a school couldn't provide the education necessary to meet your child's needs, chances are you would want the flexibility to invest with another, more appropriate, service provider – perhaps a sporting club, a leadership camp, a farm or a factory.

Above all else, you would actively advocate for an education for your child, not just for bricks and mortar, wouldn't you? And wouldn't every other Australian parent?

Has Gonski 2.0 delivered a currency that shows little regard for Australia or its future?

I suspect so.

First Published July 25, 2017

Chapter 3: Funding and School Choice

🗨 Positive Action: Adding Value to School Funding

Schools face problems. The view that money – or more of it – is the universal solution creates a lot of confusion. The Gonski school funding model hasn't disappointed in that regard. It has become less about an appreciation of Federal investment, and more about highlighting the various inequities between the 'haves and have-nots', in school sectors, and in States and Territories. The model is confusing, divisive, and highly politicised, and appears to have little chance, if any, of delivering on its original promise.

The reality is that many principals, school board members, teachers, and parents don't really know how the model works. Most schools tend to allocate government funds to consolidated revenue. In such cases, therefore, despite a formula designed to combat disadvantage, the Gonski model does not necessarily bring direct benefits to the children it targets.

Effective school leaders seek wiser ways to invest the funding they receive. They maintain a focus on their core business – that is, *learning* across the whole community.

Further, these leaders identify areas where funds have already been well spent, and find ways to replicate that success, placing themselves in an even stronger position to increase their schools' performance. This strategy also reduces what some might even regard as 'acceptable' waste.

As an effective leader, you can maximise the value of Government funding.

FIVE POSITIVE ACTIONS YOU CAN TAKE

1. View your NAPLAN results differently

Despite what you might think, NAPLAN is a powerful resource for school-wide improvement. Consider a school that has been below the national average for five consecutive years. Every year the group of students is the variable, but it is likely that the group of teachers, and the instructional leadership team or coach remain the 'constants'. Year 3 NAPLAN results do not reflect five months of schooling; they reflect three and a half years of teaching and learning. You can use your NAPLAN results to gain a better understanding of the performance and professional investment required of your team of early years teachers. Apply the same principle to the results for Years 5, 7 and 9.

2. Place your strategic focus on your whole organisation

A school's core business is *learning.* Strategic planning and subsequent actions tend to focus on the clients – that is, on student performance. This approach overlooks several areas of potential improvement. Learning opportunities should encompass all staff members and stakeholders. With a view to improvement, audit your existing strategies,

Chapter 3: Funding and School Choice

including systems, processes, resources and personnel. Develop a more effective and efficient financial review. Then you can be more confident that funding, regardless of the amount, will be spent in the best possible way.

3. Invest in family support and allied services

According to the Australian Curriculum Assessment and Reporting Authority (ACARA), a child's family background – including parents' occupations and level of schooling – has an influence on educational outcomes. If parents have a low Index of Community Socio- Educational Advantage (ICSEA) the implication is that their children will have a reduced capacity to perform well at school. In other words, ICSEA has nothing to do with your school facilities, staff, or teaching programs. This understanding paves the way for increased discretion, in terms of where your funding is spent. A greater investment in allied services is one way to target family background criteria more effectively. It also reduces the pressure on teachers to deliver services beyond their qualifications.

4. Close the gaps in your community

The wisdom of crowds is powerful, especially when your parent community boasts a range of vocational strengths. Rather than relying on one-way communications, such as newsletters or union brochures, consider providing opportunities for valuable interaction, including panel discussions, Q&A evenings, and webinars. Parents see education through a very different set of lenses, and it's important to welcome their input, as an advantage rather than a threat. Closing the gap for students involves closing the gap between their teachers and parents.

5. Turn vague intention into successful reality

Funding is like any program. It isn't personalised and it doesn't deliver itself. People do that. Great schools have brilliant leaders who are outcome driven, and whose focus is on generating porous boundaries – where funding and staff performance are effectively integrated. To personalise the goodwill of funding – regardless of its monetary value – successful educational leaders personalise staff development, targeting real needs and setting measurable objectives.

Effective leaders do not take the view that money – or more of it – is the answer. Have confidence in your capabilities, and celebrate two things: your successes, and the failures that bring about considered change. Never be afraid to abandon plans that don't deliver, even if you have invested time and resources in them. Invest wisely in your staff and your community, and you will have high-performance people, working to shape a high-performance school.

First Published October 2, 2016

Chapter 3: Funding and School Choice

Adding Value to Our Schools

Public schools are valuable assets. Most occupy prime real estate in central locations – ensuring ready access to students who live within reasonable proximity. Public schools are often seen as the heartbeat of their community. The local Church and the Scout Hall might have lost patrons over the years, but the public school continues to serve the neighbourhood, despite the fact that in some locations its site and its facilities are stretched to the limits by growing student numbers.

In 2012, the United States had a staggering 98,454 public schools. In 2015, New Zealand recorded 2,441 state and state-integrated schools, and the Australian Bureau of Statistics recorded 6,651 public schools in 2014.

Among the many challenges educational leaders must face, the primary one is student enrolments. Each year Principals and School Boards must navigate the waves of enrolments, and the impact they have on student-teacher ratios, staff employment, timetables, funding, allied services, operational expenses and so on.

Indicators such as birth rates, transitional housing, and community demographics can generally be relied on to give indicative estimates of student enrolment figures. But sudden population changes, caused by migration, for example, and the consequent increase in student numbers can occur at a faster rate than schools can manage. And

Thought Starters On Education

there's the dilemma. How can schools continue to provide the best possible education for their communities?

According to *The Age* (October 10, 2016), the number of students attending Victorian public schools will reach one million by 2020. Some public schools won't be affected, and the construction of new schools will ultimately prove a solution. Principals and School Boards in major growth corridors, however, are already working hard to deal with massive overcrowding.

Staggering is their current tool of choice, and it seems to be doing the job. Schools are compensating for overcrowding with staggered start and finish times, staggered playtimes, and staggered lunch breaks.

Two factors help. Legislation does not mandate start and finish times. Teachers' face-to-face classroom time is no more than 22.5 hours per week. This means there is ample room for flexibility to start the school day earlier and finish it later. Where schools have tried this, the management of student growth has been achievable. Staggering is a terrific approach to an otherwise complex issue.

Is it possible to build on the concept of staggered days and extend it further? Could we consider staggering the school year?

For Victorian students the school year is currently 40 weeks. Teachers, like most professionals, are employed for 48 weeks and are entitled to 4-weeks leave *per annum*.

Chapter 3: Funding and School Choice

Principals have the authority to approve staff leave, and in some overcrowded schools, which have successfully introduced a more flexible school day, perhaps staggered annual leave for staff, and staggered holidays for students, might be worth further exploration.

Could staggering be the catalyst for reviewing other educational and social issues? What about spending more time on targeted teaching, or increasing flexible work options? Could it reduce peak traffic, or avoid high season travel costs during holiday times? Could schools become employment hubs for small businesses – for the teaching of English, sport and recreation, art and technology classes, or for support groups, to name just a few? Could public schools become less competitive and more locally focused? Could Victoria begin the global reform of schools and education, in finding local solutions?

Today, 1,524 Victorian public school buildings lie dormant for 12 weeks of the year. That's a great many valuable resources sitting idle for almost a quarter of the calendar year.

Rather than simply ask 'Why?' perhaps we should be thinking of ways to maximise their value, and then ask 'Why not?'

First Published 11 October 2016

Chapter 4: Genuine Parent Relationships

For centuries, parents have carefully chosen highly regarded individuals – including people of faith, philosophers, and the well-educated – to contribute to the education of their children. Today, although some parents still invest in subject-specific tutors, compulsory schooling has replaced the parent as the direct employer, and the teacher has replaced the carefully chosen tutor.

How well do you know the individuals who teach the children in your local school?

● ● ●

Thought Starters On Education

Genuine Partnerships

In my workshops, I'm constantly asked: "What's the best approach to stop parents questioning the learning and teaching taking place in schools?"

It's the wrong question. Parents have every right to know and understand exactly what is happening in schools.

Much better questions are:

- What changes are needed to make sure parents are better informed?
- How can we ensure genuine parent-teacher relationships?

And, more importantly:

- What do parents need to know in order to 'take the lead' in their child's education?

Schools don't raise children – parents do! Schools provide the service of teaching, which assists parents in the education of their children.

For parents to take the lead in their child's education, they must be encouraged to learn more about what is expected of their child's teachers, the strengths teachers bring to their roles, and the support available to help them provide the service for which they are qualified.

Chapter 4: Genuine Parent Relationships

Whatever falls outside their qualification or capability shouldn't be a burden on their shoulders; it should be placed in the capable hands of other, more appropriate, service providers.

In genuine partnerships, parents and teachers share fundamental principles, maintain boundaries, and show respect, support and honesty. They also understand that neither home nor school alone has what it takes to raise 'the whole child'. That's something they do together.

First Published 15 Feb 2018

Thought Starters On Education

The Highly Regarded Educator

The morning my eldest daughter started school, I did two things. I greeted her teacher with warmth and respect. Then I burst into tears.

The scene was familiar. I'd been in many like it, since I was in my 20s. But this time my role was different. Then, I was the teacher, and childless. Now, I was the parent, and handing over my 5-year-old daughter, whom I had adopted from Thailand just 18 months earlier. It was awfully distressing. First, because my daughter was reluctant to let go of me. Second, because I knew I could no longer protect her. Third, because the concept of parents putting blind faith in teachers, which I had previously experienced as a professional, was now a personal and grave reality for me as a mother.

From the moment we become parents, the full responsibility of raising our children rests squarely on our shoulders. Parenting is no easy task; neither is the task of navigating the many services that help us raise our children. Whatever your personal circumstances, though, you have a voice. You can choose your general practitioner, your private health care provider, your specialist, and infant health service. You decide on your playgroup, your babysitter, and childcare service. Navigating and selecting services becomes a major part of your responsibility as a parent. You are the decision maker.

Chapter 4: Genuine Parent Relationships

But then, one day, our children commence compulsory schooling. We hand them over to individuals we know very little about. And the older our children get, the less likely we are to know about the various teachers they have.

But it hasn't always been this way.

Long before schools were established, wealthy parents sought tutors to build knowledge, positive judgement and wisdom in their children. Confucius (551 BC – 479 BC), regarded as the world's first private tutor, was a master at this, and developed trusting relationships – first with parents and then with his students. An invitation to tutor a child was an invitation to nurture ethical citizenship in the next generation. It was considered a great honour.

For centuries, parents have carefully chosen highly regarded individuals – including people of faith, philosophers, and the well-educated – to contribute to the education of their children. Today, although some parents still invest in subject-specific tutors, compulsory schooling has replaced the parent as the direct employer, and the teacher has replaced the carefully chosen tutor.

How well do you know the individuals who teach your children?

First Published January 23, 2018

Thought Starters On Education

Hold Back the Creep

What would you do if you heard schools were taking children from their parents? It sounds like an outrageous question, doesn't it? Nevertheless, it's one I would like you to take seriously. Every day decisions are made in schools and classrooms. Parents and teachers might agree with most of them; some, however, result in the 'removal' of parents from their children's lives.

In September 1990, the United Nations Convention on the Rights of the Child – a statement about the care and assistance of children – came into force. Comprising 54 articles, its overarching preamble states: '…the family as the fundamental group of society and the natural environment for the growth and well-being of all its members and particularly children, should be afforded the necessary protection and assistance so that it can fully assume its responsibilities within the community'.

In other words, the statement acknowledges parents' right and responsibility to raise their children. However, it is also understood that services are available to assist them in doing so. Schools fall into this category and their assistance is limited to the services they can provide.

Herein lies the dilemma.

The Convention on the Rights of the Child and its interpretation must be watched closely and debated widely. For

Chapter 4: Genuine Parent Relationships

families to be afforded assistance and protection, what services should schools provide for families? More important, what limits should be placed on school services?

Some services essentially represent a social or political 'creep into schools.' Often the process happens subtly, and rarely raises a major alarm. However, before long, the fundamental rights of the family have been eroded. The *Safe Schools* program and the proposed *Doctors in Schools* initiative are just two examples that compromise the boundaries between home and school.

In the past, visiting school nurses, in-house school counsellors and psychologists have been welcomed into the school environment. On the surface, they appear to be of valuable assistance to families. On further reflection, have these services inadvertently become part of a slow creep toward the removal of children from their parents?

Two things must be defended: parental voice and parental choice – in conjunction with the fundamental and clearly understood principles central to a teacher's role.

Everyone has a direct or indirect relationship with schools. What happens in schools – programs, services and their outcomes – affects us all. Regardless of your relationship with schools, stay informed and be involved. Above all else, don't be afraid to speak out on behalf of the fundamental group of society – the family.

First Published 21 November 2017

Thought Starters On Education

Trumping Australian Schools

Australian education is in dire need of overhaul. If you need evidence, look at the 2015 exam results recently released by the Programme for International Student Assessment (PISA).

The PISA exam, which is administered every three years, measures 15 year-old students' abilities, in 73 countries. It is the world's leading external exam, and provides a snapshot of a nation's education. In 2015, Australia was ranked 10th in science – down from 8th position in 2012; 12th in reading – down from 10th; and in mathematics ... yes, down again – from 17th to 20th place.

Despite the billions of dollars spent, year after year, we have been in consistent decline since 2000.

These latest results raise essential questions about our educational system and our global ranking, and suggest the need for dramatic change, if we are to achieve improved educational outcomes for our students and, indeed, for our nation.

Dramatic change calls for dramatic action. We mustn't be afraid to go deep – to the root cause of the stagnation and decline. Neither should we resist the repurposing of some of the greatest initiatives previously presented by both major parties.

Chapter 4: Genuine Parent Relationships

In 1788, the First Fleet sailed into Botany Bay. Among the first arrivals were 36 children: 19 were the offspring of the marines and 17 were from convict parents. Children of the privileged and the poor lived together in the penal colony, under one rule of law. We had our first charter of justice, and it articulated law and order, but failed in its provisions for education.

As our colonies grew, so too did the need to address the significant failure to provide education. There were attempts to provide schools for the children and stem the vagrancy that came with rapid population growth. Trial systems were implemented, and there were the inevitable struggles for control, and loss of trust. The result was a major fallout between government, parents, and faith groups.

The political battle that ensued pitched man against man, colony against colony, culture against culture, and faith against faith. Land, power, legislation and opportunity were all part of the balance – or imbalance – and a centralised public system was born. Schools and schooling became big business.

In matters of education, the USA is similar to Australia in many ways. It shares its powers between Federal and State Government, and it has seen a decline in PISA performance. There have also been some outstanding reforms, designed to counter lack of choice, and offer opportunity and progress to every child; none of these reforms has survived the poison of political ego.

Thought Starters On Education

Australia and the USA have both public and private schools. Each has denominational institutions, home schooling, international schools, and virtual schools. Australia has selective entry public schools, and the USA has 'magnet' schools. Although they are public, these schools are highly competitive and highly selective. They're renowned for their special programs and high academic standards.

The USA also has a growing charter school movement.

Charter schools are public but, as the term implies, they have the freedom to chart a more autonomous course, reducing the top-down influence of Federal and State governments. Charter schools are independently operated by community organisations or for-profit companies, who receive tax dollars and private sponsorship.

The challenge for both the USA and Australia is to create a decentralised, flexible school system, where Federal and State governments put a bipartisan approach to greater choice and greater autonomy ahead of political power.

In Australia, the current funding model is shaped by the Gonski reforms. It links funding to children's needs, but funds still go directly to the schools. In some US states, however, school funding is based on a 'voucher system', where funding follows the child. This system fosters greater choice, and access to more autonomous, specialised schools, including magnet and charter schools.

This approach has attracted Donald Trump's attention.

Chapter 4: Genuine Parent Relationships

Some of the things Trump has to say about school reform in the USA raise questions for Australia, too:

1. Let them choose

'As President, I will establish the national goal of providing choice to every American child...' Mr Trump said.

Should Australia consider a voucher system, or similar, so as to provide greater opportunity for all children, particularly the disadvantaged, to attend the school of their choice?

2. Let schools compete

'Who's better off, the kids who use vouchers to go to the school of their choice, or the ones who choose to stay in public school? All of them. That's the way it works in a competitive system', Mr. Trump said.

Should Australia introduce charter schools, giving local schools the opportunity to choose their area of expertise, thereby attracting expert teachers and talented students?

3. Portability and local school boards

'I'm not cutting services, but I am cutting spending. We're going to be cutting tremendous amounts of money and waste and fraud and abuse', says Mr. Trump.

Should Australia consider an 'Educare' system – similar to Medicare? The same accountabilities would apply, and funding would be available for all children to receive effective literacy, numeracy, and values education. If schools offered specialist education, it would fall under a 'user pays' or voucher model?

Thought Starters On Education

The essence of education can be described as the imparting of knowledge, positive judgement, culture, and well-developed wisdom from generation to generation. Australia was founded as a Judeo-Christian nation and, it has to be said, also founded on an omission, which has seen education used as a political football rather than a time-honoured gift.

The USA also has a scattered system, with pockets of success and deep wells of failure. Perhaps we have something to learn from Trump's enthusiasm. Perhaps it's time for Australia and the USA to work in unison, to provide education systems that value, and offer, diversity, choice and opportunity. Perhaps it's time to be human first, politically correct second, and to develop first-rate education systems that cultivate the 'Australian Fair Go' and the 'Great American Dream'.

Australian education has gone backwards. This trend is reversible. All that is required is the will of our people, our politicians and a genuine belief in what's possible. Only one question remains. How hungry are we?

First Published December 18, 2016

Chapter 4: Genuine Parent Relationships

Challenging the Norm

Schools usually expect parents to be active in support of their child's learning and to engage in school initiatives – with regard to homework, committees, working bees, fundraising and social events. You could say it's the norm.

However, this expectation is based primarily on the more traditional family unit, generally with one parent as income earner and one – usually the mother – as homemaker.

The evolution of the modern family, however, challenges this expectation. Other additional issues also have an impact on a family's ability to participate, or to engage, according to the 'norm'.

Disability is one of these. The issue of disability in schools very much focuses on the child, but parents are directly affected too. In the USA, over 4 million parents live with disabilities and 1 child in every 10 has a disabled parent.

Hearing impairment, physical disability, mental illness and intellectual disability don't necessarily prevent individuals from becoming parents; neither do they prevent parents from raising their children well.

Parents who have disabilities, however, might find themselves precluded from participation in a school community if their circumstances are misunderstood, or if perceptions create further disadvantage and isolation.

Thought Starters On Education

In the USA, over 4 million parents live with disabilities and 1 child in every 10 has a disabled parent.

Schools that serve their communities well, do not judge parents. They actively seek counsel from external services so that all parents, regardless of circumstances, have every opportunity to participate as and when they can.

First Published 12 March 2018

Chapter 4: Genuine Parent Relationships

🗨 Parents: Be Aware, Be Assertive, Be the Voice

Don't ever apologise for demanding the best for your child.

We live in a democratic society that gives us a voice by virtue of our right to elect our government representatives. Schools have a similar representative system. Elections are held to determine who will represent the school community on the school council or board.

Parents have a right to know precisely what takes place in schools.

And rightly so. It is understood that a school's responsibility is to educate its students, but what is not always articulated clearly is that education involves not only teaching, but also the provision of advice.

According to the Victorian Department of Education, principals and teachers are frequently called upon to advise students. It recommends that teachers, when doing so, should limit themselves to areas within their professional competence and avoid giving advice in areas unrelated to their role or where they might lack experience.

What then constitutes a teacher's 'professional competence' or 'experience'? If teachers deliver curriculum content to students, is it implied that they have the professional

Thought Starters On Education

competence to provide students with advice related to that content?

Consider these 4 examples – taken from real situations in Australian schools:

1. Teachers are using vibrators – devices used for sexual stimulation – to show 14-year old students how to put on condoms. Do these teachers have the professional competence to deliver this content, or to advise students on what to do if, for example, a condom were to break?

2. The definition of 'asset' has been widely accepted to mean: 'a resource that is owned or controlled by an entity, which has a future economic benefit'. In textbooks referred to by VCE students studying accounting, this definition has been amended by deleting the word 'owned'. Do teachers who have never practised as accountants understand the implications of this change in the 'real world'? Are they equipped to advise students on the establishment and control of entities?

3. More than 16,000 science teachers have signed up to access a Year 9 resource that teaches students how to lobby for environmental issues and discuss who to vote for, based on the issue of climate change. Do these teachers have the professional competence to blend science and politics in a bipartisan manner, or to advise students – who are not even eligible to vote – on political issues of any kind?

4. Christian schools are introducing gender neutral uniforms and providing forums for students to discuss

Chapter 4: Genuine Parent Relationships

their 'transgender' identity. Do teachers have the professional competence to challenge Christian values, or to advise students on matters of gender that contradict Christian values?

Schools operate in a democratic system, where the people elect the government, and the school community elects its school boards or councils. How well informed are you about what takes place in your child's school? How willing is the leadership at your child's school to consult with you, and other parents, on any and all matters that have an impact on your values, morality and political standing? What right do schools have to deliver content or advice regarding matters of which you have not been made aware?

Most importantly, why doesn't the Victorian Department of Education website state that principals and teachers do not have the right to advise students on any matters without parental permission. Surely this would help distinguish professional competence from opinion; it would certainly provide better protection for principals and teachers, with regard to duty of care.

Don't be afraid to ask questions. Don't ever apologise for demanding the best for your child. Assert your right to know what's really going on in Australian schools.

Be the voice that democracy expects you to be.

First Published 20 August 2018

Thought Starters On Education

Advocating for What's in Common

What's the difference between the best school in the worst street and the worst school in the best street?

The answer is simple: its community.

A community is a group that holds particular attitudes and interests in common. A school is not only part of the wider community; it is a community of itself. This means education flows within and beyond the school boundaries. Each member of the community, however, must clearly understand the shared attitudes or values, and the interests of each child must be paramount.

A genuine parent-teacher relationship can achieve all this. It starts with an understanding, on both sides, of what a school has to offer.

A school is not only part of the wider community; it is a community of itself.

Parents have every right to understand all that relates to schooling – particularly the faith and/or educational philosophy the school follows and offers. Teachers have the right, and the freedom, to foster the agreed faith and educational philosophy and to challenge expectations that are contradictory to community agreement.

Chapter 4: Genuine Parent Relationships

Whether you're a teacher, a parent or a guardian in a school community, don't be afraid to ask questions. These are your children or students. You have every right to advocate for the education you want them to have. The key is knowing exactly what the school values, and precisely what it can contribute.

First Published 20 March 2018

Thought Starters On Education

Parents Treated Like Rubbish

Parents of children who attend Victorian public schools are being treated as worthless.

The State Labor Government has introduced laws giving schools the power to silence parents and remove their rights.

Concerns over the *Safe Schools* and *Doctors in Schools* programs have encouraged parents to speak out – and so they should.

Some implications of these programs are:

- Girls as young as 12 will be able to obtain the contraceptive pill from doctors stationed in government schools.
- A teacher's opinion can be sought to help a doctor assess a case and potentially override any parent refusing consent.
- Children are being provided with Internet links to learn how to use sex aids.
- Masturbation is taught in class.
- Pre-schoolers are being groomed for sexuality and gender education.

However, removing parental rights doesn't stop here. The State Labor Government has introduced additional laws

Chapter 4: Genuine Parent Relationships

giving the Minister of Education total control over who teaches our children, and where.

If a child is away from school, charges can be laid against parents.

A principal can prepare a certificate of absence to be used in proceedings against parents.

Parents who choose to home school their children must provide detailed plans of what will be taught.

Attendance officers have the right to enter the family home to inspect the home school.

The State Labor Government has also introduced laws that essentially give public schools parental responsibility:

Principals, teachers and other workers in a school have the same rights as parents over any child.

Anyone working in a Government school must apply the principles of secular education. At the same time, however, they can follow any leader of any philosophy, religion or faith.

Parents Victoria, an organisation paid to advocate for the rights of parents, is backing the Victorian Labor Government.

What is happening in Victorian public schools can no longer be ignored or left to others to address. Any laws that

Thought Starters On Education

are binding in Victorian public schools are binding outside the public education sector, and outside Victoria.

Every parent, including teachers and principals who are parents, must act now.

Here's what to do:

- Share this article on social media and urge your contacts to do the same.
- Contact your local newspaper and urge them to report on this matter.
- Speak with your school principal and demand answers.
- Speak with your School Council president and demand answers.
- Form a parent lobby group and develop a plan of action to: Protect your children; Support teachers and principals to protect your children; Research Victorian law; Boycott the Victorian Labor Government; Write to news outlets.
- Get your children involved. Keep them close, and keep them safe in your presence.

First Published 7 August 2017

Chapter 4: Genuine Parent Relationships

Power of the Big G

During the 1950s, Victorian schools introduced out of hours 'Mothers and Daughters' evenings. Their purpose was to provide health and sexuality education, delivered by those qualified to do so.

Today, health and sexuality education is delivered during school hours but, unfortunately, not always by people who are appropriately qualified.

Doctors also attend schools. They can treat 'mature minors' – students under 18 years who are deemed mature, i.e. those who can consent to their own medical treatment. The State government, via the schools, has the right to override parental rights, and to ignore completely any requests from parents for their rights to be heard.

These changes haven't happened overnight. Small incremental changes since the 1950s mean that parents and teachers have gradually relinquished their respective parental and professional rights to government.

Two questions arise.

The first is this: Why would parents and teachers wish for a situation such as this?

Thought Starters On Education

The second, more important question, for those teachers who are also parents: What remaining rights – if any – do you have?

Be alert. Government – The Big G – is watching over you (and your children's health and sexuality education).

First Published 24 November 2018

Chapter 5: Authenticity

Authenticity isn't about following the status quo, the latest trends, or the major influencers.

Neither is it about being defiant and different, simply in order to stand out.

Being authentic is to be, to do and to say what is true for you, whether you're the same as someone else, or different from everyone.

• • •

Thought Starters On Education

A Sprinkle of Difference

My Christmas tree is like no other in the world – it's authentic. I've collected ornaments from places like Santa's Workshop on the Arctic Circle, Times Square New York, Kathmandu and hundreds of other places I've had the good fortune to explore. They now decorate my tree, hanging beside ornaments lovingly made by my daughters, and the finished result is one of the best conversation pieces of the festive season.

As I purchased each ornament I knew it was just one of many that looked much the same. But when it was added to my collection, it became a special contribution to my unique festive masterpiece. My tree is a tapestry, woven with reminders of times and places, which also stimulates others' special moments and memories.

In so many ways, we are also much the same as others. But if every similarity we shared were packaged together in the same way, there would be no unique or authentic quality in any one of us.

Authenticity isn't about following the status quo, the latest trends or the major influencers.

Neither is it about being defiant and different, simply in order to stand out.

Chapter 5: Authenticity

Being authentic is to be, to do and to say what is true for you, whether you're the same as someone else, or different from everyone.

The Christmas season is a wonderful time to remember all that you are and all that you are not. It's a time to stop selling yourself short and embrace being yourself. You're not meant to be like everyone else, and they are not meant to be just like you.

To be authentic requires a sprinkling of difference. And that difference is what makes you uniquely *you*.

First Published December 18, 2017

Thought Starters On Education

Reality: Yours, Mine, Ours

Cast your mind back to 2001, to one of the most heart breaking events of recent times – the attacks of September 11. Where were you when you heard the news? How did it affect you?

I was in New York that day, the impact on me was very real.

Just four days earlier, my five-year-old daughter and I had moved from Melbourne to New York. I was living my dream – doing the two things I loved best: being a mum and inspiring school leaders to raise the bar of the teaching profession.

On the morning of September 11, I had commenced work – consulting with teachers in a large Brooklyn public school. As I walked past the office, I heard an administrator yell: "Oh my God, a plane has hit the Pentagon".

Within minutes I was thrust into taking a lead, with the principal, operating with calm and order, but with no details other than that the school was in lockdown.

I thought immediately of my own daughter, in school, several suburbs away. I had no way of reaching her. Was a leader watching over her, just as I was helping to care for 900 children and dozens of staff? Did she know that I was desperate to be with her? Was she as scared as I was?

Chapter 5: Authenticity

The day was a surreal blur. As the morning's events continued to unfold, we responded to departmental instructions, consoled staff who had family and friends working in downtown Manhattan, and co-ordinated security pick-ups for panicked parents desperate to have their children close. Amidst all the activity, we maintained a positive and professional front – encouraging teachers to continue as best they could, and distracting the children until we knew more.

I finally reached my daughter at 5pm. She was the last remaining child at her school. Both shocked and elated to see me, she said, "I thought you were gone and I would have to find a new mummy". It rocked my identity to the core.

Over the years I have listened to hundreds of people share their reality of that fateful day. I've comforted a stranger on a subway, hearing her desperation of the loss of her husband, struggling to breathe while beginning to make sense of her new reality. I've listened to stories of those waking up the morning after, millions of miles away, believing they were experts in the event. I've listened to friends too frightened to fly, to conspiracy theories, to anger, to heartache and hope.

My story, my daughter's story and every other story I've heard are real.

For everyone who experienced 9-11 a unique reality exists. The real world is in the here and now. It's in classrooms, living rooms, workplaces, dole queues and on the streets.

Thought Starters On Education

The real world is the one each of us are living, regardless of where we are living it.

There is no such thing as preparing someone for the real world or for the 21st century. There is, however, much to be said for preparing someone for the many things they may encounter when going about life, wherever they are, whenever they do, for whatever purpose they have.

When schools talk about preparing students for the real world or the 21st century, are they admitting that life inside school is neither real nor valid?

I don't believe that to be the case.

However, I do believe, that school is simply one part of someone's reality – whoever that may be, whenever they are there.

First Published 7 May 2018

Chapter 5: Authenticity

To Be of Service

The joy of festive gatherings is meeting interesting people. I recently met a first responder – a fireman. We spent time comparing workplace experiences and were intrigued by a particular professional element we had in common – the bell.

Teachers get out of bed each workday confident in the familiarity the school bell brings. The start of learning and teaching, the 30-minute morning tea break, the 1-hour lunchtime, and the end of the school day are all signalled by the bell. Teaching professionals provide a service, safe in the knowledge that assessment, teaching, behaviour management, meetings, regular breaks and peer collaboration are all part of a safe and familiar routine.

My fireman friend and his colleagues, however, wake each morning, never knowing what lies ahead. More importantly, they can never know whether they'll return safe, or injured, or make it home at all. Attending fires, gas leaks and car accidents, calming the dying and being front and centre in life's catastrophes are the pieces that potentially make up their daily routine. For them, the bell brings a different type of familiarity – providing a service that could cost them their lives.

For them, the bell brings a different type of familiarity – providing a service that could cost them their lives.

Thought Starters On Education

The joy of festive gatherings is more than meeting interesting people. It's a reminder that the bell is a symbol of something sacred. How blessed we are to have extraordinary people willing to risk their lives so that we too can be of service.

First Published December 5, 2017

Chapter 5: Authenticity

 The Principal Act

Researchers consistently agree that teachers are far more likely to have a large and positive impact if they:

- Know what needs be taught
- Teach
- Monitor what has been learned
- Adapt their teaching as necessary

In other words, if teachers competently carry out the tasks they are paid to do, their positive impact will be greater.

This is stating the obvious. But what if they don't? If teachers have deficits in any of these four key measures, however, there is very little, if anything, principals can do.

A report compiled by Australian Council for Educational Research (ACER) paints a very telling picture of this very issue. Specifically, it notes that principals believe they lack influence or extensive authority with regard to their own teaching staff.

Here's a snapshot showing the percentage of Australian principals who feel they have no authority to affect the teaching profession – their own staff – in 5 key areas:

- Reviewing teacher performance 40%
- Prioritising professional learning 50%

Thought Starters On Education

- Determining staffing profile 75%
- Dismissing poor performers 90%
- Rewarding high performers 98.8%

Australian principals are charged with the management of multimillion-dollar budgets, and the provision of quality education, but 90% know there is little they can do about poor performance among their staff.

If that's not bad enough, 40% of schools have no mechanisms to distinguish between high and poor performers. Their principals believe they have no authority to review teacher performance and, even if they had, 50% believe they have no authority to determine the professional learning required to lift poor teacher performance.

As terrible as this might seem, there is some good news. The statistics above come from a report published in November 2011.

Now, Australian principals who lead schools with multimillion-dollar budgets do have a level of control over the services their schools provide.

They are involved in professional learning, they have the authority to prioritise on-site professional learning, and they can distinguish poor performers from high performers.

What they still can't do, however, is motivate the unmotivated, or break away from a deep and influential bureaucracy

Chapter 5: Authenticity

– that is, of course, unless they are personally willing to face dismissal or accept rewards, by placing their own professional performance on the line.

A difficult decision perhaps, but one that could lead the way to reform, and greater choice, in all areas of employment in Australian schools.

I suspect that could that have a widespread and positive impact on principals, teachers, parents, students and the wider community.

First Published 6 November 2018

Thought Starters On Education

To Guarantee Continued Freedom

When we form views and beliefs we are usually influenced by facts and opinions. All too often, our views are also shaped by emotive immediacy and we make choices with little regard for the potential consequences.

A recent vacation to Cambodia provided me with a stark reminder of why we in the West must never be complacent about our freedoms, and why we must come to terms more fully with the notion of consequence.

Less than 50 years ago, and just 7,000 kilometres from Australia, between 1.5 million and 2 million people perished. They were executed, or died as a result of starvation, disease and overwork. One man was responsible. While working in a respected position, as a school teacher, he callously planned a social engineering initiative. His name was Pol Pot.

Here is a snapshot of the material on display at one of Cambodia's Killing Fields, where mass graves and human remains bear witness to the human carnage the country suffered for this man's ideology.

> 'Communism is the principle regarding the common ownership of wealth in which there is collectivity and equality. The idea of Communism is to try to establish a new society, which bears no class struggle; it tends to link with socialism'.

Chapter 5: Authenticity

In Cambodia, the ideology was to have "no class struggle", and for all to be equal. Is this an ideology that resonates with you? In Cambodia, the price was mass murder. What price would you pay?

A short drive from the Killing Fields is the former school that became the S-21 detention centre, where approximately 20,000 people were imprisoned and died. Today education is again the key to its existence. It tells a story of a barbaric genocide, so that such horrors will never occur again. And its main audiences are the survivors and the descendants of those who were tortured or killed. Inside S-21, panels displaying the facts of history span the rooms and corridors.

It tells a story of a barbaric genocide, so that such horrors will never occur again.

Some examples:

> 'This clique of Criminals wanted to transform Cambodian people into a group who knew and understood nothing and always bent their heads to carry out the orders of ANKAR (KAMPUCHEA Communist Party) blindly. They educated and transformed the young people and adolescents, whose hearts are pure, gentle and modest, into odious executioners who dared to kill the innocents and even their own parents, relatives or friends'.

> 'This clique of Pol Pot Criminals burnt the market place; abolished the monetary system; eliminated national culture; destroyed schools, hospitals, pagodas, and priceless monuments such as Prasat Angkor which is a source of pure national pride. They did whatever to get rid of the Khmer

Thought Starters On Education

character and transform Cambodian soil into a mountain of bones and a sea of blood and tears, which were deprived of cultural infrastructure, civilization and national identity, [and] became a desert of great destruction that overturned the Cambodian society and drove it back to the Stone Age'.

This year marks 100 years since the end of the enormous carnage of the First World War. Far less than 100 years ago were the Great Depression, the carnage and destruction of the Second World War, and the Korean and Vietnam Wars. Many of our elders suffered and fought for the freedoms we have and, dare I say, take for granted; some are still with us. They fought and defeated the very ideology that Cambodia faced during the Pol Pot era.

Sadly, the same ideology – for all to be equal – is alive and well today, in our Parliament, our workplaces, our classrooms and our homes.

Is this an ideology that resonates with you? Are you guilty of being in agreement with an individual, purely because of their position or title – only to learn later that the alleged facts and opinions, concealed their real agenda?

Our future relies very much on our past. It depends on the passing on of accurate accounts of events, sacrifices and changes that have ensured our Western way of life.

The consequences of any equality debate are often identified only when it's too late. Your knowledge, energy and wisdom are essential, to ensure that the people who serve

Chapter 5: Authenticity

us do so for the sake of equality that guarantees our continued freedom.

First Published 29 January 2018

Chapter 6: Pedagogy and the Teaching Profession

In professional circles, teaching is often better known as pedagogy. A simple definition of pedagogy is 'the art and science of teaching'.

All teachers have their own unique pedagogy or 'professional DNA'. In other words, every teacher has an individual and unique approach to delivering the curriculum – that is, what is intended to be taught and learned.

● ● ●

Thought Starters On Education

Can We Detect a Heartbeat?

Schools play a vital role in our lives.

We all have recollections of the great, the good and the not-so-good experiences of our school years. And, for many, schools are considered the bedrock of childhood and the heartbeat of a community.

It could also be said that a community is only as good as the school that leads it.

The Civics and Citizenship is a learning area of the Victorian curriculum. It highlights the influence that schools have on our students and our communities. With its emphasis on 'contemporary' or present day views of society, one of its key aims is for students to develop 'the capabilities and dispositions to participate in the civic life of their nation at a local, regional and global level'.

In other words, our schools encourage students to be concerned with the affairs of the community, rather than devote themselves merely to the pursuit of personal interests.

But how do we measure the value of this teaching? By comparing just a few historical and present day civic duties, it is fair to say that whatever measure is used, there is room for concern.

Chapter 6: Pedagogy and the Teaching Profession

- In 1949, Victorian schools established Christmas appeals to benefit children of ex-servicemen and women, and children in out-of-home institutions. By 1967, more than 115,000 toys had been donated by school-age children.

- In 1968, 435 Junior Red Cross Clubs operated in public schools across Victoria. Students made toys, raised money and visited lonely and elderly citizens.

- In the same year, the Victorian and Commonwealth Governments worked together to provide 339 free language courses for adult migrants throughout Victoria. Most of the classes were held in government schools.

- The Australian Charities Report of 2014 reported that government invested $42 billion in charities, in the form of government grants; the highest single portion (36%) of this investment went into education.

- In 2014, the Victorian Department of Education and Training (DET), as result of the Royal Commission into Family Violence, introduced a Primary School Nurses Program, investing $51 million into the DET School Student Services division. The Program received 6,774 disclosures from students; just 280 cases of family violence were dealt with.

- In 2016, an average of $6,000 per teacher was spent on professional development. During that year, DET employed 41,570 full-time teachers – with a bill of $249,420,000 for professional development in Victorian public schools.

Thought Starters On Education

Could it be that the curriculum's emphasis on 'contemporary' issues has played a key role in the demise of civics and citizenship in our communities? Have schools themselves unwittingly become devotees of the pursuit and promotion of personal self-interest?

Schools continue to play a vital role in our community. The question is: have they lost their heartbeat?

First Published 4 September 2018

Chapter 6: Pedagogy and the Teaching Profession

Pedagogy to Puppetry: Who's Pulling the Strings?

In professional circles, teaching is often better known as pedagogy. A simple definition of pedagogy is 'the art and science of teaching'.

All teachers have their own unique pedagogy or 'professional DNA'. In other words, every teacher has an individual and unique approach to delivering the curriculum – that is, what is intended to be taught and learned.

Pedagogy is influenced by many factors, not the least of which are the latest research and the current trends in education. And, looking closely at its definition – as both 'art and science' – it's easy to appreciate the influence teachers can have on their students.

The art and science of pedagogy

Art is considered to be the expression or application of creative skill and imagination, which has emotional power. Think for a moment what it takes to engage, and hold, the attention of 24 restless five-year-olds, or 22 hormonal 14-year-olds. Teachers use their skill and imagination every day to maintain a functional level of work in their classrooms.

Science involves the study and observation of the physical and natural world, and experimentation in behaviours. Teachers constantly make judgements about student behaviours, achievements and needs. They continually make decisions about how they will change their teaching – or experiment with various methods – to make sure students' experience the desired outcomes within the curriculum.

Having the freedom to do these things gives teachers power and gives them choice. In a profession that has become increasingly bureaucratic, how can this freedom be encouraged, welcomed, and valued?

Extinction of pedagogy

The truth is, it cannot. Pedagogy, as we know it, is sliding rapidly towards extinction. The art and science of teaching are being replaced by formulae to be endlessly replicated.

Teachers no longer prepare to offer a unique experience and way of being. Instead they are expected to operate out of a 'common language' and a 'common understanding', which ensures their 4.5 hour teaching day looks identical to that of every other teacher at the same year level or school.

Will the future see teaching as simply a craft – and teachers as puppets?

The erosion of talent and expertise is increasing with the use of what is known as 'direct teaching'.

Direct teaching is the strict patterning of teacher behaviour, through the provision of lessons that are written as scripts for teachers to follow, word for word, with little or no room

Chapter 6: Pedagogy and the Teaching Profession

for dialogue between teacher and students. Lessons can be prescribed to a point where students' questions are predicted, and the teachers' predetermined answers also provided. In other words, there is little need for teachers to think. Direct teaching is an attempt to place quality controls on the delivery of the curriculum, on teaching, and on learning.

No-one would dispute the need to include the fundamental foundation skills that must be taught – particularly in literacy, numeracy and classroom behaviour. They are critical. There is a very strong argument, however, for the boycotting of direct teaching that takes away from teachers their creativity, their intellect and their potential to be themselves.

Consider the implications of a system where education is controlled by teachings from a textbook that offers no opportunity for critical thinking, dialogue or rebuttal.

Direct teaching is a valuable commodity for bureaucracies. It effectively erodes the professionalism of teaching. It allows greater opportunity to pull the educational strings. It replaces 'personalised teaching' with mere 'puppetry'.

Consider the implications if we fail to understand this, and fail to see what's really going on in our nation's schools.

First Published 28 August 2018

Thought Starters On Education

🗨 Flushing Out Failure

You can't necessarily equate qualifications with capability. In terms of 'trained' teachers, this has, unfortunately, never been more true.

The results of a national research project that gathered data over a 5-year period from 2012-2017, indicated the greatest frustration experienced by capable teachers and principals was being forced to work with, and protect, incapable colleagues.

Last weekend, media outlets reported that Australian Universities continue to enrol in their training courses students who have failed Year 12. If these students are to become tomorrow's teachers, we can fairly predict that the number of teachers who lack the ability to fulfil their responsibilities will increase.

Australian Tertiary Admission Rank (ATAR)

Let's be clear. These university students have not only failed Year 12, but some have performed exceptionally badly, with ATARs in the 20s. What does this mean?

The Australian Tertiary Admission Rank (ATAR) is given to students at the completion of Year 12. It's an estimate of the percentage of the student population an individual has outperformed. For instance, students receiving an ATAR of 60, means they outperformed 60% of other students.

Chapter 6: Pedagogy and the Teaching Profession

Universities are accepting students with an ATAR rank of less than 20 – in other words, students who have outperformed only the lowest 20% of their cohorts.

These latest reports also suggest Education Ministers and opposition spokespersons can, or should, effect the changes necessary to avoid such a situation. Although this might be true to some degree, two critical voices are missing.

The first is that of our principals and teachers. Why do capable school principals and teachers accept graduates from these Universities as their employees and colleagues? Teaching simply cannot be considered a profession when complacency, or fear, overrides any mechanism to flush out failing teachers.

The second voice is that of school councils and boards, which include parent representatives. Why do they allow their schools to accept and protect incapable employees? Parent representatives voice opinions on behalf of every parent in their school communities. Surely parents want only the best and brightest to teach their children.

School leadership sits at the centre of a complex web of relationships that determine whether a community, or society, flourishes or fails.

If our children are not taught by the very best, what kind of society will Australia become?

Thought Starters On Education

There is no excuse for anyone directly involved in Australian schools to remain silent on this or any other matter that degrades performance, and potentially brings the nation to its knees.

There is no excuse for allowing school leaders – whether principals, school councillors or board members – to accept anyone who is incapable of educating our children as a member of staff.

Say no to inadequate standards. Say yes to capability. Say it loudly and clearly. Then flush.

First Published 14 August 2018

Chapter 6: Pedagogy and the Teaching Profession

Is Teaching Really a Profession?

The word 'teacher' can be traced back to the Greek term *deiknumi*, which means 'to point out' or 'to show'. Great philosophers, including Aristotle, Socrates, Confucius and, more recently, Rudolf Steiner, were educators and private tutors of the highest order. Their work was to understand and 'to point out' what it is to be human, and how to live a peaceful and fulfilling life. They concerned themselves with issues of ethics, spirituality, wisdom, faith, politics and tradition.

Over time, learning with a trusted, private tutor-philosopher, has evolved into the teaching of students en masse in formal places of learning – schools.

What exactly was to be taught in these places, and who would be qualified to teach there, have also gone through an evolutionary process. The consequence: the introduction of formal qualifications, and of teaching as a profession.

Are teachers today anything like the great philosophers of the past? Do they concern themselves with issues of ethics, spirituality, wisdom, faith, politics and tradition?

National Teaching Workforce Report

A 2014 report on the *National Teaching Workforce* [1] provided statistics on the qualifications held by those in the teaching profession. Of 45 subject specialisations

Thought Starters On Education

– meaning those requiring study for 3 years or more – politics was studied by less than 3% of student teachers and religious studies was studied by less than 20% of student teachers. Ethics, spirituality and tradition were not listed.

Consider these issues as well:

- Every subject area involves the need to read, write, speak, listen or record one's thinking. Yet less than 50% of Australian teachers have English as a specialisation.

- Schools receive financial loadings to cater for students who speak a language other than English. Yet less than 10% of teachers are qualified to teach these students, and less than 10% of teachers have themselves studied a second language.

- Schools receive financial loadings for children with special needs. Less than 9% of teachers, however, are qualified in special education.

- Students are allegedly being prepared for the 21st century, and for a technology-centred future. Yet less than 11% of teachers are qualified to teach Information Technology and less than 1% of teachers are qualified in career education.

- The Safe Schools Program – an anti-bullying program that includes gender and sexuality education – is available nationally. However, less than 7% of teachers are qualified in behaviour management, less than 6% are qualified in psychology, and less than 6% are qualified in civics and citizenship.

Chapter 6: Pedagogy and the Teaching Profession

If 'teacher' is connected with *deiknumi*, which means 'to point out' or 'to show', and if a profession is a paid occupation that involves prolonged training and formal qualifications, then what do these figures tell us about our teaching profession?

Over time, learning with a trusted, private tutor-philosopher, has evolved into the teaching of students en masse in formal places of learning – schools. What is taught in schools and who is qualified to teach there have most certainly gone through an evolutionary process.

What are our teaching professionals qualified to teach? Are they educators of the highest order?

Despite increased investment in schools, the introduction of a national curriculum and national testing, and a consistent focus on student outcomes, these figures indicate relevant qualifications in specialised areas are sparse.

Could it be that, despite the introduction of formal teaching qualifications, Australia is becoming a knowledge-less society?

And, despite the claims, is teaching in the 21st century really a profession?

[1] NATIONAL TEACHING WORKFORCE DATASET DATA ANALYSIS REPORT JUNE 2014 COMMONWEALTH AUSTRALIA

First Published 28 May 2018

Thought Starters On Education

Commitment to Capability

It's not uncommon for parents to place a high level of trust in teachers. It makes sense to assume that teachers, as professionals whose purpose it is to work with children, possess immense knowledge, wisdom and integrity.

However, the teaching profession is no different from any other. Every school has its share of outstanding teachers, who take their job seriously and provide a service above and beyond expectations. And, as in any other profession, there are also those with lesser degrees of capability or commitment.

If you went to a hairdresser you would expect to be satisfied with the service; otherwise, you wouldn't go back. Similarly, you would feel it necessary to have a trusting relationship with your medical practitioner, and make accurate disclosures, so that effective assessment, treatment and ongoing care could take place. The same can be said for the teaching profession.

In workshops, during the last 5 years, I have often asked teachers and principals 2 specific questions:

1. With hand on heart, would you say you'd be comfortable if your own children's education were entrusted to any and all of the teachers you know?
2. If, to continue in your capacity as a teacher, you were given the autonomy to lease your classroom,

Chapter 6: Pedagogy and the Teaching Profession

and provide a pedagogical service you believed in, would you do it?

No-one has yet answered 'Yes' to the first question. To the second question, most say 'No', but some are curious to know more.

What does this tell us about the teaching profession, how it is viewed, and how teachers see themselves? To what degree do parents and teachers speak out to ensure teachers are not seen as a one-stop shop for all things educational?

When will we appreciate fully that many teachers are parents too? Surely, as parent and teacher, they are demanding a quality teaching profession for their own children?

First Published 10 April 2018

Thought Starters On Education

 The 'Some' of Us

It's not uncommon for parents to place a high level of trust in teachers. It makes sense to assume that, as professionals whose purpose it is to work with children, all teachers possess immense knowledge, wisdom and integrity.

However, the teaching profession is no different from any other. Every school has its share of outstanding teachers, who take their job seriously and provide a service above and beyond expectations. And, as in any other profession, there are those with lesser degrees of capability or commitment.

And, let's not forget, teachers have personal lives, too. Some have experienced trauma, hardship, and family violence. Some are bullies and some have been bullied. Others have children with criminal records, drug addiction or disability. Some are highly successful in other fields of endeavour. And some struggle to balance work and family life, just like the parents whose children they serve.

The point I'm making is simple. The 'sum of teachers' is a completely different concept from 'some of the teachers'.

No system or policy, no change in legislation or funding model can produce any desired result until every teacher – just as every child – is considered on merit, capacity, strength, network of support, and need.

Chapter 6: Pedagogy and the Teaching Profession

And only then will 'difference' be the much-needed descriptor for equality.

First Published 26 February 2018

Thought Starters On Education

💭 Evolution Instead of Revolution: Thinking About Personalised Teaching

In Shakespeare's *King Lear*, when Edmund realises his villainous acts have returned to haunt him, he says, 'The wheel is come full circle, I am here.' (5, iii, 171)

As an extremely motivated mature aged graduate, I had quite a bit of Edmund in me. I clearly recall how I eagerly shared new ideas and strategies with colleagues, and became more than a little frustrated when none of my elders seemed to be listening. I came to realise that the ideas weren't really new – they were just packaged differently.

Needless to say, it took me no time at all to learn that reinventing the wheel was definitely on the school curriculum and still is.

Thought leaders, researchers, governments, and other stakeholders – the influencers who determine how schools operate, succeed or fail, and how they are viewed – collectively keep the wheels of perceived innovation in motion. Teachers and school communities are motivated by these innovations, but they are equally frustrated by the constant changes – the rephrasing, rebranding, or regurgitation of what should or could be done to improve student outcomes.

Chapter 6: Pedagogy and the Teaching Profession

It's no surprise that the constant negativity surrounding student performance has produced a new breed of stakeholders. Civil society now dabbles in innovative products, programs, and calls to action, all the while raising funds to ensure a secure place in the education landscape. With so many commercial, and other interests, it's little wonder that, as we dance in its tracks, the wheel makes a full revolution, and what we thought was past comes back to haunt us.

Of all the stakeholders in the field, it is only the teachers who meet students eye-to-eye, day-to-day, in the classroom. Teachers must rely on their instinctive capabilities to address 'deficits' in student performance across a wide and varied cohort, all the while meeting a further demand: to demonstrate a capacity to adopt, and apply, the latest innovations. And each great innovation is recycled and replicated sevenfold to seventyfold, until, before long, evidence suggests it hasn't produced the intended result and is therefore deemed a failure.

Since the late 1940s, UNESCO has played a major role in maintaining a global focus on 'basic education and literacy', the result of which has led to ongoing debate about approaches to literacy methodology, assessment, and intervention in the early years. Phonics, as a particular example, has been in and out of favour as a method of teaching letters and sounds. In fact, it is an essential component, alongside word study, and vocabulary enrichment, in developing competency in English orthography.

Thought Starters On Education

To continue debate over the value, or otherwise, of phonics and what it means, negates its necessary contribution to the process of becoming literate – that is, to understand and be understood.

So once again the wheel turns. We invest even more, as we research, rephrase, rebrand, rework, or replace ways to achieve our primary purpose: seek solutions, and keep the 'whole child' at the centre of all our intentions and justifications.

What if we were to turn this thinking on its head and saw initiatives as an opportunity to refine and personalise our teaching practice?

What if our collective political energies were spent on nurturing evolution – from teacher into powerful educationist? Old ways of doing would become new ways of thinking and being, for all teachers, along their continuum of professional capacity. Would it then be possible for every researcher, every innovation, and every brilliant idea to be heard and actioned – not because policy demands it, but because teachers actively choose to adopt an individualised approach to teaching – owning their own pedagogy?

What would be the impact – a greater professional respect, greater responsibility for an evolving course of action and an accountability to self with respect to vocational responsibility? Could these better serve teachers and in turn our students, our colleagues and the wider community?

Chapter 6: Pedagogy and the Teaching Profession

What if we mirrored the concept of 'the whole child', and supported every teacher as 'the whole educationist'?

What if we regarded deep learning, and personal and spiritual development as more important than the collection and mediation of data that do not capture the whole child anyway?

What if student outcomes could be viewed through the evidence of their teachers' own pedagogical values and actions, contributions, and network of support, rather than the focus be only on children's achievement or deficit?

What if a teacher discovered that being an educationist, and being responsible for students, was not his or her calling and, as a result, could celebrate new ways of learning, and transition to a more suitable career?

What if unique and powerful educationists were genuinely honoured? They would be highly paid professionals, and teachers would lift their game, to become educationists, or choose to contribute in a less lucrative supporting role.

Is this performance leadership in action? Or is it simply the pipe-dream of an extremely enthusiastic mature aged graduate, who some, thirty years later, still excitedly shares ideas, but this time with a little more wisdom?

Having the benefit of more wisdom I am determined to be heard. Reinventing one wheel at a time, one child at a time, one teacher at a time, is far too slow, and will continue to leave schools to a fate that Shakespeare understood:

'We know what we are, but know not what we may be.'
(*Hamlet*: 4, v, 43)

First Published 2 September 2016

Chapter 7: English Language and Literacy

Although it is true there are many philosophical approaches to learning and teaching, there is no escaping one critical need: a focus on the fundamental principles of the English language. Language underpins everything – concepts, ideas, the making of meaning and all human communication.

● ● ●

Thought Starters On Education

There's 'Something' About Education

How much do you value education?

This question is extremely complex, and one that raises even more questions, including a very basic one: What does 'education' really mean?

Let's consider this as a definition:

> *Education is the wealth of knowledge acquired after studying subject matter, or experiencing life lessons through instruction or composed literature, which provides an understanding of something.*

This definition suggests, quite rightly, that we are all educated. We are certainly not, however – and we never can be – educated in the same something. We all have different ways of receiving, processing, producing, sharing and using what we know, do and understand.

Consider these four levels of capability: craft, skill, trade and profession:

1. To have a **craft** is to demonstrate a competency – generally using your hands.
2. A **skill** is acquired through making deliberate and sustained efforts to carry out complex tasks.

Chapter 7: English Language and Literacy

3. Competency in a **trade** requires special training in manual work.
4. To have a **profession**, you must have acquired mastery of complex knowledge and skills, through study and practical experience, over a sustained period of time.

Each of these levels requires study, instruction and the relevant literature. In other words, these levels represent four different ways of acquiring education. They have, however, a crucial factor in common.

In order to know, to do and to understand, a craftsman, a skilled labourer, a tradesperson and a professional must, to varying degrees, have a level of competency in the English language.

The measure of an education, then, could be said to be a measure of language competency.

We are not all educated in the same 'something' – but our education depends on something vital.

Let's return to the original question: How much do you value education? Perhaps the value we place on education can be the measure of our own willingness to invest in that certain 'something' – the English language.

First Published 18 September 2018

Thought Starters On Education

Self-inflicted Digital Incarceration: Be Careful What You Hope For

There are two things that should be beyond question. First, that Australia's common language is English. Second, the inherent value of our English language is that it gives us the ability and freedom to communicate with depth and full understanding.

Without that ability, messages conveyed or received can become rather murky or misinterpreted. There's also the risk that directives or reforms are not fulfilled, or not sufficiently questioned to determine their merit or intent.

Digital education is a case in point.

This year marks the 10th anniversary of the Digital Education Revolution (DER) in Australia. It was a $2.2 billion project, aimed at, 'changing teaching and learning in Australian schools, to prepare students for further education and training; and to live and work in a digital world'.

In 2011, a survey was conducted to identify the success of this project. Of 9,435 schools, just 175 schools, or 0.018%, responded. These schools were encouraged by 'changes in students' access and use of computer engagement, and preparation for a digital world'.

Chapter 7: English Language and Literacy

In stating it was 'changing teaching and learning in Australian schools', was the DER aware of historically poor response rates by schools, and therefore also aware there would be little, if any, evidence of revolt from schools with regard to the DER?

When the DER was introduced, 90% of Australian schools reported a computer:student ratio of worse than 1:2, justifying the investment in providing one computer for every student in Years 9–12. Seven years later, 25% of WA schools acknowledged their devices were more than four years old. Maintaining state-of-the-art digital access, via purchase or lease, would now be up to parents in WA, and all other parents across the nation.

In stating that it was 'preparing students for further education and training,' did the DER really mean its investment was temporary, and that parents would become the major investors in digital communication?

Today, digital devices include cell phones and tablets. Continuous access to information, whether accurate or otherwise, is the new social currency. Moment-in-time monitoring and reporting is the new school currency.

We post, we 'like', we tweet, we abbreviate. Every time we share a post or selfie, we believe we are popular, socially engaged beings.

In stating that it was 'changing teaching and learning to prepare students to live and work in a digital world,' did the DER realise that competency in the English language would be compromised by the 'monitoring' of peers and the 'reporting in' of each and every one of our own movements?

Could it be that the Digital Education Revolution has been a greater success than was ever hoped for (or feared)? Have the ability and freedom to use language been compromised? Have we, in fact, been the engineers of a self-inflicted digital incarceration?

First Published 25 June 2018

Chapter 7: English Language and Literacy

Raising Poor Spellers

Having spent 30 years passionately working in education and publishing, I am appalled at my capacity to succumb to the seduction of technology, and the self-inflicted embarrassment I suffer as a result.

My personal library is home to hundreds of articles and books I have either authored, commissioned or edited. It houses wonderful works by colleagues I have taught, coached and mentored. I value each piece, and feel blessed that in some small way I contributed to each author's message. I consider these works as part of my story too, because they demonstrate the evolution of my calling from teacher to educationist, and educationist to agitator.

My email account, on the other hand, is home to atrocious spelling and grammatical errors. They live, I am sorry to say, not in my draft file or inbox, but in my sent file. I send emails to a diverse range of professional people, whom I respect immensely. To insult them with my poor spelling is bad enough, but to think they might consider me complacent or incompetent is worse – particularly given the work I do.

To read, comprehend, and produce English – the most widely recognised language on the planet – is an accomplishment we simply cannot take for granted. Whether it's chalk on slate, pen on paper, or fingers on keyboards, with every recorded word we are the authors of our lives, shaping how others view us and, as I have learned, how we view ourselves.

Thought Starters On Education

Every day I face the challenge of empowering fellow educationists to see themselves as leaders in the acquisition of the English language. I constantly adapt my suite of tools to improve my performance, and to nudge, energise and encourage teachers to be the risk takers we expect our students to be.

I've learned so much, over so many years, that there's no excuse for my poor use of English in emails. The over-emphasis on technology – in my life, in schools, and in all our lives – has also taught me a great deal.

The top five lessons I've learned:

1. Use keyboards just like quill and ink. They are tools for writing. How they are used and respected depends on the writer. Keyboards can be turned off, just as the quill can be put down.

2. Respect every email you receive. Take time to provide a considered response. If you don't have time, don't hit the send button.

3. Poor conventions affect how a message is comprehended. Your readers will always infer something. So be kind to yourself. Do more with less, and be sure the inferences made are focussed on your intended message rather than conventional error.

4. Embrace your partnership with the English language. See it as your pathway to stronger relationships.

Chapter 7: English Language and Literacy

5. Be willing to learn and, more importantly, be willing to know nothing. Stand in the same shoes as your students, your readers, your peers, and your motivators.

The true value of the written word is to learn from the genius of great authors. Imagine if Socrates, Shakespeare, Charles Dickens, Ralph Waldo Emerson, or Sigmund Freud, scribed illegible, misspelled and poorly constructed manuscripts. Would their provocative and life changing messages have missed the mark?

Genius

'Genius', in its purest meaning, is the natural, innate, creative ability each one of us possesses. Whatever our own unique brand of 'genius', whatever our individual insights or contributions, we owe it to ourselves, and to those who read what we offer, that the written expressions of it are the best they can be.

Docendo disco scribendo cogito – Latin for "I learn by teaching, think by writing" – is my professional creed. So if I am to carry the title of 'educationist', then I must not be seduced into poor excuses: less time; 21st century blended learning; technological advancement; or work overload.

No, I must be the example of what I value most – to understand and to be understood.

First Published 3 August 2016

Thought Starters On Education

Literacy, Technology and the 21st Century

My grandfather – or Gramps as we loved to call him – lived to the age of 97. He went to his grave feeling that he had failed, that he wasn't literate, and that he hadn't kept up with change. But Gramps' achievements were not measured by tertiary qualifications or preparation for life in the 20th century.

He dropped out of school in the second grade, to bring in an income to help the family. He lived through a number of wars, the Great Depression, the introduction of television, the first landing on the moon, and the invention of the mobile phone. He raised four beautiful children, and was known as Gramps to 14 grandchildren and 31 great-grandchildren. Gramps' name appears in an historical publication of Carlton and United Breweries. He was a non-drinker, but he was one of the first men in Australia to drive a truck, rather than a horse and cart, to deliver beer. He served during World War II, repairing aircraft in Papua New Guinea, and later he was chief gardener for his local council – a role that required him to drive a tractor.

In 2002, just before his passing, UNESCO delivered a new statement on literacy: 'Literacy is crucial to the acquisition, by every child, youth and adult, of essential life skills that enable them to address the challenges they can face in life, and represents an essential step in basic education, which

Chapter 7: English Language and Literacy

is an indispensable means for effective participation in the societies and economies of the twenty-first century.'

My Gramps lived a full and rich life. He embraced technology and change. By any definition, he was a literate man. His life epitomised the 2002 UNESCO vision.

We should keep in mind, though, that innovation and change have been rolling through human history since the time of the hunters and gatherers. We must make sure that the seductive call of technology does not tempt us away from other necessary skill sets. Their loss would be too great an expense to the community.

As your child's school career continues, technology will evolve, and schools will be challenged, and seduced, by computer coding, new reforms and research opportunities.

And neither should we forget that the best way to help our children acquire a love of the English language, and build vocabulary, is through conversation. Face to face, eye to eye interaction is the most powerful method of all. Replace television with conversation, smartphones with books, and encourage pen and paper rather than computers. Talk to your children often and leave the formalities of becoming literate to the professionals.

First Published 27 March 2018

Thought Starters On Education

Moving Forward with Fundamentals

John Wooden, the great UCLA basketball coach, is known for two things: winning seven consecutive NCAA championships between 1967 and 1973, and being one of the greatest inspirational leaders, basketball has ever produced. The first lesson he taught his players was to tie their shoelaces. His reasoning was: "This is a game played on your feet. If you get blisters, you can't play the game".

For him, it was about getting the groundwork right, and laying the foundation for his players to develop all the skill sets they needed to become champion basketballers. The same can be said for becoming literate.

Language underpins everything – concepts, ideas, making meaning and communication.

To become literate, children need to recognise and produce symbols – the 26 letters of the English alphabet. They must be able to manipulate them, to construct words and combine them with others to create meaning. To do this accurately, they must know the different sounds and patterns letters can make – on their own and in combination with others. And they need to be aware that parts of words can have their own meaning too.

We all have our own unique bank of words – more commonly known as vocabulary. We access or recognise vocabulary whenever we read and listen. We produce and

Chapter 7: English Language and Literacy

use our bank of words whenever we speak and write. And when we produce them accurately we make sure others can create meaning from our intended message.

While it is true there are many philosophical approaches to learning and teaching, there is no escaping the critical need for the fundamental principles of the English language. Language underpins everything – concepts, ideas, making meaning and communication.

So next time you hear discussions about the 'basics', replace the word with 'fundamental principles'. It's about getting the groundwork right, and laying the foundation for our children to develop all the skill sets they need to become competent, confident communicators.

First Published 5 February 2018

Thought Starters On Education

'Either-or' Means Everyone's a Loser

When we use 'either-or', we are emphasising a choice between two alternatives. The expression is widely accepted in debates related to education. It makes it clear that the options in question cannot exist, or be achieved, at the same time.

A common and frequently reported 'either-or' situation relates to debates about the 'phonics' method and its value or otherwise in early reading instruction. This is often incorporated into the 'back to basics' debate. Another common issue is class size, where one side argues the positive or negative impacts on student outcomes, and the other argues the irrelevance or minimal impact of class size. And let's not forget the 'haves and have nots' argument in the school funding debate.

Ideas and concepts are the true power behind progress, innovation, civil society and education.

To take the 'either-or' approach as a means of arguing or lobbying for any philosophy or outcome in education is cause for extreme concern. It implies that an idea or concept is wrong (or right) depending on which side you are sitting in the 'either-or' debate. It suggests there are winners and losers.

Chapter 7: English Language and Literacy

This couldn't be further from the truth.

Ideas and concepts are the true power behind progress, innovation, civil society and education. Ideas and concepts offer us genuine platforms that give rise to robust debate, research and investment. Limiting ourselves to an 'either-or' approach leaves little room for the exercise of non-partisan agreement, fairness, independent thought or legitimate equal opportunity. We all lose.

If the 'either-or' agenda were to be removed from all education debate, and if, instead, ideas or philosophies were viewed through an optimistic transdisciplinary lens, what might education look like?

Perhaps, to begin, there would be a thorough investment in English – in its 26 symbols, their flexibility and their use. These symbols are the passport to independence, self-discipline, responsibility, and further education. The same can be said for numeracy and the principles associated with the numbers 1-10. Without the ability to use and understand these fundamental tools with an agreed degree of automaticity, our opportunities are limited and our dependency increases.

'Back to basics', or what might be better described as 'moving forward with fundamentals' is a necessary investment and enabler for the flexible use and access of everything else education offers. Class sizes, funding, the fight for equality, and any other 'either-or' can do little for the individual, the teacher, the student or civil society unless there is first a thorough investment in the English language.

Funnily enough, these 'basics' require self-discipline, responsibility, independence and further education. And, there's no 'either-or' about that!

First Published 24 September 2018

Chapter 7: English Language and Literacy

The Teaching of English: A Primary Concern

In 1886, a guide book for the teaching of elementary (Primary) English, was published in New York. Beginning with the basic learning symbols – the English alphabet – and ending with proofreading marks – the symbols used to edit manuscripts – the publication included 100 lessons on prepositions, conjugations, particles, interjections, adverbs and clauses, to name a few.

For those reading it today, it is an interesting example of how the fundamentals of English were taught in logical progression, as pupils mastered one skill and moved on to the next.

There are no similar publications used in Australian schools today. Instead, teachers navigate a vague national curriculum – or its amended equivalent – and source potential content from a myriad of websites, products and recommendations. They oversee learning goals set by the students themselves as part of a popular self-directed approach to learning and teaching.

The logical process of skill development and the expectation that all children – other than those genuinely identified with learning difficulties – will achieve a required level of mastery have essentially been removed from Australian schools.

Thought Starters On Education

High-frequency words are those regularly used, regardless of the content being explored. Examples include: of, and, was, I, then, because, the, have, know and would. The NSW Department of Education states: 'Knowing 100 of these frequently used words gives a beginning reader about half of the words they (sic) need for reading'.

Here's an example from the Australian Curriculum (AC) of expected outcomes for students in relation to what are known as high-frequency words:

- Foundation: Know how to read and write some high-frequency words.
- Year 1: Use visual memory to read and write high-frequency words.
- Year 2: Use knowledge of letter patterns and morphemes to read and write high-frequency words.
- Year 3: Recognise and know how to write most high-frequency words.
- Year 4: Read and write a core of high-frequency words.

How many high-frequency words does the Australian Curriculum understand there to be?

Which high-frequency words are to be read and written, and in what time frame? How many words are implied in 'some' in Foundation, 'most' in Year 3 and 'a core' in Year 4?

Chapter 7: English Language and Literacy

The Organisation for Economic Cooperation and Development (OECD) states that primary education usually begins at ages five, six or seven and lasts for four to six years. In Australia, primary education lasts for 7 years and, as can be seen, students have five years to read and write a core of high-frequency words – possibly a minimum of 100.

But why isn't this stated clearly? If our children are encouraged to sing songs and chant rhymes by practising, memorising and learning by rote, surely the same strategies, or similar persistence, can be applied with regard to a specific number of specific essential words from our English language – right from the very first year of primary school.

It turns out the OECD also states that 'programmes at the primary level generally require no previous formal education'. Could we interpret this to mean children can progress through the primary years with no pre-requisites from the previous year? Is the Australian Curriculum (AC) conforming to OECD standards? Has Australia's investment in primary education been made with the stark ultimate goal of passing our children on to secondary schools, regardless of their ability?

In 1886 a guide for the teaching of English was published. Its purpose was to provide a logical pathway to competency for those teaching and learning the English language. It's a fine example of what basic education in the English language was and, indeed what it could be again.

Thought Starters On Education

To achieve it, we might have to stand outside the shadow of the OECD and create our own definition of 'primary education'. First, however, we must determine what we already know, what we don't yet know, and exactly what knowledge we expect future generations to acquire.

First Published 30 July 2018

Chapter 7: English Language and Literacy

Handwriting: Gone With The Wind

A bundle of letters from a 'pen pal' – my best friend at primary school. A collection of Christmas cards from students I taught 30 years ago. Birthday cards from loved ones, some now deceased. They have no material value, but to me they are priceless. Why? Because they are handwritten messages.

Do you have similar treasures?

Handwriting, or symbolic representation for others to interpret, is uniquely human. It's a skill that has been passed down through the ages – evolving from pictographs first drawn on rocks, to the abstract symbols that became the English alphabet we use today.

Handwriting involves linguistic, cognitive, perceptual and motor components, all of which must be coordinated into an integrated action. And, although one might not distinguish handwriting from other forms of writing – in terms of using legible, correctly formed letters to communicate thoughts and ideas – handwriting is special.

The real power of writing by hand is in the craftsmanship. Each letter – uniquely formed – is as individual as the writer's DNA and fingerprint. Every stroke of the pen enables us to express that which is ours alone – our unique signature.

Thought Starters On Education

Today, many argue that writing by hand has been compromised by the use of digital devices and anonymous keystrokes. However, its demise could have begun well before the latest technological wave of 'one device for every child' washed over us.

In 1972 the world's first national level environmentalist party – the Values Party – was formed in New Zealand. In the same year, the United Tasmania Group was the first Green Party in the world to run a candidate. It was also the year blackboard and chalk in schools suddenly became a health hazard.

Teachers no longer worked from the front of the room. Group work and roving became the new norm. Universities replaced Teacher's Colleges. Reading began to take precedence over writing, and 'free writing' took precedence over grammar and spelling. The formal teaching and practice of writing declined, and so did the ability to record thoughts and feelings.

And, 10 years from now, if the so-called conservation movement achieves its ambition of having an 'electricity system based on 100 percent renewables', the dominance of the digital device over the pen and paper might well be complete.

Today, in the signature line, X can literally 'mark the spot'. By one simple keystroke an individual can lose the ability to express something that represents individuality.

Chapter 7: English Language and Literacy

Tomorrow, the use of another simple keystroke might also be in decline, if wind-generated power replaces the switch.

Could it be that the forces behind the so-called conservation movement and the changes in education really represent a protest movement against free thought and enterprise?

First Published 3 July 2018

Thought Starters On Education

Who's Hijacking the English Language?

Since the establishment of various Education Acts during the late 1800s, Australia's colonial school curriculum relied on books – referred to as readers – and monthly school newspapers, to establish and supplement skills in reading and writing. The focus was on English literature, history, and non-denominational moral values.

The teaching of English became the responsibility of schools. The learning of English was the responsibility of every citizen.

Becoming literate includes the ability to recognise and produce symbols – the 26 letters of the English alphabet. It's also about the capacity to manipulate these letters, to construct words and to combine them with others to create meaning. In other words, becoming literate is about becoming a user of words, or vocabulary. Our everyday experiences continue to influence the vocabulary we acquire, understand and use.

Although the English language is more or less the same today as it was during the late 1800s, the teaching and learning of English has taken on a life of its own.

For example, schools have unwittingly allowed themselves to be hijacked by philosophies that offer an 'either-or'

Chapter 7: English Language and Literacy

approach to the essentials of phonics and comprehension. As a result, they have been left with a deficit – either in phonics or comprehension, at best, or, at worst, in both.

Herein lies the dilemma.

The strategic direction taken by an individual school is the responsibility of the school council, which is made up of parents, teachers and community representatives. In other words, the school council is responsible for ensuring the effective teaching and learning of English.

Could it be then, that the political focus on phonics, comprehension and the teaching of English is misguided? What is required, perhaps, is a sharper focus on those responsible for driving a school's strategic direction.

English hasn't really changed since the establishment of Australian public education in the late nineteenth century. Teaching English remains the responsibility of schools and learning English is still the responsibility of every citizen.

First Published 19 June 2018

Thought Starters On Education

Essential Fundamentals

This year, the nationally agreed education agenda for Australia – the *Melbourne Declaration on Educational Goals for Young Australians (2008-2018)* – is in its final year. The agreement, between all States and Territories, was made to ensure Australian schools provide the best educational outcomes for all children.

Here's a list of areas in the lives of all Australian children, in which the governments of the day (2008) considered it absolutely necessary for schools to be involved:

- intellectual
- physical
- social
- emotional
- moral
- spiritual
- aesthetic

Two years prior to this agreement and its implementation, Australia ranked among the top 10 countries in educational outcomes for 15-year-olds, in Science, Reading and Maths *(PISA 2006)*.

In 2015, seven years after the agreement, Australia's performance dropped to 10th in Science, 12th in Reading,

Chapter 7: English Language and Literacy

and 20th in Maths. In 2017, according to United Nations Children's Fund *(UNICEF),* Australia ranked 39th out of 41 countries for quality education.

So what went wrong?

In Australia, the first laws and the subsequent Constitutions for each of its States were based on values that came from Judeo-Christian traditions. When public schools were established, they too were guided by those same values.

The *Melbourne Declaration*, however, makes no mention of this. Its focus instead is on global citizenship, anti-discrimination, Asia Literacy, technology, equality and indigenous affairs.

If Australia is to reclaim its place among the top 10 countries for educational outcomes, perhaps the next set of educational goals should begin with an agreement on the fundamentals: a respect for and appreciation of difference; competency in the English language; and an assurance that Judeo-Christian values remain woven into the fabric of our schools, our laws, and the Australian way of life.

First Published 19 February 2018

Thought Starters On Education

Writing Slump in Australian Schools

Australian schools have been rocked by yet another blow. 2017 NAPLAN test results reveal poor performance across the nation. Early indications from the data are that students' writing skills have gone backwards over the last 6 years.

No surprises here. Below is a 16-point list of issues that contribute to Australian students' poor performance in writing.

1. NAPLAN reviews student performance, not teacher performance.
2. Teenagers are moving out of secondary school into University with writing skills that are less than adequate for them to become teachers.
3. University courses do not 'bridge the gap' in English for trainee teachers.
4. Course content in Universities is too broad, leaving graduate teachers ill prepared and more likely to demonstrate poor performance in the workplace.
5. The English language has been enriched and developed for centuries; the teaching of English, however, continues to be 'watered down' in Universities and consequently in schools.
6. Many schools over rely on 'reading levels' to claim students' development in English.

Chapter 7: English Language and Literacy

7. Many schools do not have accurate tools to assess spelling, grammar or writing.
8. Most teachers do not trust the results their colleagues provide in relation to students.
9. Teachers use their judgement to assess student performance; there are no agreed skills or knowledge criteria, however, to validate their judgements.
10. After qualifying, teachers are not required to undertake any further professional development in English.
11. There is an endemic over reliance on, and investment in, products that offer prescribed lessons.
12. Support staff increasingly take on teaching roles – particularly with students who have fallen behind year level expectations.
13. Schools invest too heavily in technology; they invest more in technology and books than in pen and paper.
14. There is more profit for businesses in promoting technology and books than in pen and paper.
15. Insufficient time is spent on learning to write.
16. Most teachers do not themselves regularly practise the writing genres in which students are expected to excel.

To improve student performance, there is one immediate step we can take. We must demand an acceptable standard of skill, and insist teachers reach it, as a minimum requirement. Until such time this is achieved, no amount of school funding or spending will be enough to break out of the slump.

First Printed 2 August 2017

Chapter 7: English Language and Literacy

🗨 What Are Our Children Really Worth?

The NAPLAN test – Australia's National Assessment Program for Literacy and Numeracy – is just weeks away. And with it will come the usual media coverage of the arguments against its value. We can expect the usual issues to be raised: funding, student stress, teacher burnout, and comparisons between States and Territories.

Who or what is driving the desire to expect less, know less and offer less to our citizens?

In Australia, compulsory schooling evolved between the 1880s and 1900s. The nation's first census, held in 1911, collected data on citizens aged under 5, 5 to 9, 10 to 14, 15 to 19, and over 20 in the following categories:

- Those using the English language (whether they could read and write, or read only)
- Those using a foreign language only (whether they could read and write, or read only)
- Those unable to read

Compulsory schooling didn't initially mean all students were required to attend school, but it resulted in the national goal of universal literacy.

Thought Starters On Education

'Life's true value is in contemplation, conversation and care.'

In the USA, the first education law was in 1642, and coincided with the introduction of periodic checks on student progress in reading, writing and comprehension. Parents were given no choice. Their children had to be educated, and they could be fined or lose custody of their children if deficiencies in English were found.

In the United Kingdom, the first grammar schools were established during the 600s, some 1270 years before education was made compulsory.

What can we learn from this very small historical sample? What did our early proponents of education aim to achieve? Perhaps by valuing education and literacy, they were expressing the value they placed on their children and their future. Surely, that's worth measuring.

First Published 24 April 2018

Chapter 8: Politics and Schools

Increasingly, public school leaders throughout the world are becoming political advocates. They often breathe life into extremely dangerous social policy – whether deliberately or unwittingly. Some have even become part of the worldwide movement towards the demise of nurturing and the death of parenting.

Public school leaders have power and influence – and rightly so. The important question is this: does their power nurture the hopes and dreams of the families they serve, or further their own political agenda?

• • •

Thought Starters On Education

Political Correctness: Honestly?

Some say political correctness is a movement for the insecure. Many claim it's a cancer that has penetrated our schools and compromised our children's future. At best, political correctness (PC) is dishonest.

Some points to consider:

Independent and Catholic schools were founded on Judeo Christian values. State owned public schools were founded on the same values. The centuries of belief, contribution and commitment, that went into the institutions that remain standing today, still matter. PC is dishonest.

Public schooling was established on the principle of 'equal opportunity for all to be educated'. Commitment to this principle has been replaced by a cry for 'equality'. There is, however, no clearly articulated benchmark for equality. PC is dishonest.

Life in the 21st century requires innovation and strong leadership, but protected complacency in school bureaucracies outweighs risk, responsibility, high performance, experience and wisdom. PC is dishonest.

When the strident demand for 'gender neutral' entitlement in Judeo Christian schools is met, then values have been compromised. PC is dishonest.

Chapter 8: Politics and Schools

'Everyone can win at everything', is the mantra. Non-academic students pass Year 12 to be saddled with tertiary debt. PC is dishonest.

Childcare workers are educators. What, then, are stay-at-home parents? PC is dishonest.

Women outnumber men in the education sector. Yet there is no cry for a quota of male employees. PC is dishonest.

Political correctness in schools is dishonest. It is a cancer. A movement for the insecure.

There is, however, a simple solution: the introduction of Independent PC schools.

Let's see how many Australians are willing to invest in that.

First Published 15 November 2018

Thought Starters On Education

The Historian in Each of Us

Living in Western civilisation, we are part of an extraordinary story. We inhabit a time in history that offers us countless opportunities to be our true selves. While we live in the present moment, we can dream about the future, and recall our past in unique ways – including the reasons we did or didn't achieve all of our dreams.

The truth that lies at the heart of our life journey is testament to our unique presence. The truth of our recorded history, however, is a balance between our 'embellished' life, and a more humble, literal account.

And, when someone else relates our life journey, chances are it's no longer our life at all, but a fantasy about what it should or could have been.

Australian schools and universities today have three essential responsibilities:

1. To teach the history of Western civilisation with accuracy.
2. To ensure criticism of any version of Western civilisation involves open, robust and respectful dialogue.
3. To foster the desire to write, with accuracy, versions of our own lives – Western civilisation's future.

Chapter 8: Politics and Schools

Reading factual and fictional texts provides valuable understanding about our lives and those of others – past and present. The same can be said for writing history using factual and fictional genres. When schools and universities nurture these opportunities, individuals thrive and history flourishes.

The one true thing about history is that it is created in every single moment. If we accept this as truth, Australian schools and universities have one more essential responsibility – to capture the truth of the moment, flush out the embellishments and falsehoods of the past and own the opportunities of the future.

After all, each one of us is a historian. We are all in control of what is to come – a future that is nurtured by our accurate recollections of the past.

First Published 11 October 2018

Thought Starters On Education

Are You Smarter Than a 12-year-old?

How well do you know the Australian Constitution?

According to the *Australian Curriculum* (AC), Year 7 students (12-year-olds) who reach the *Achievement Standard* are able to 'explain features of Australia's Constitution, including the process for constitutional change'.

They can also identify the ideas, values and principles that underpin Australia's political and legal systems, and 'explain the diverse nature... and... shared values' of contemporary Australian society. Really?

What precisely is contemporary Australian society?

According to the *Civics and Citizenship* section of the *Australian Curriculum* (AC) Australia is a 'secular democratic nation with a dynamic, multicultural, multi-faith society and a Christian heritage'.

Interesting!

The *Australian Curriculum* (AC) fails to provide: a definition of 'secular'; any statistical information regarding the number and names of different faiths; or any compulsory reading that contains a balanced and accurate historical

Chapter 8: Politics and Schools

account of the nation's Christian heritage. These key words are absent from its glossary of terms.

This raises many concerns – far too many to address in one article.

Let's try to scratch the surface, nevertheless, and begin with 'multi-culturalism'.

Australia's cultural, political and legal systems are based on fundamental Judeo-Christian values and principles. Its citizens have the freedom to express and celebrate those unique values and principles – on condition they do not contravene them.

Australia is a Judeo-Christian culture that willingly invites citizens of other cultures to belong. This is not multi-culturalism.

With regard to 'secular' – what exactly does it mean? When society permits halal certification and the wearing of Islamic headscarves, or acknowledges Christmas Day and Yom Kippur, is that consistent with a 'secular' Australia?

Does the complete removal of God and religion from the public sphere mean a total separation of church and state? Is secularism a dilution of religious belief and practice – as in the maintaining of marriage, but with the relinquishment of its true meaning? Or is it a blending of many religious beliefs, including Islam and atheism? In other words, is Australia a religiously plural nation?

Thought Starters On Education

We must teach wisely, because our way of life, and indeed our Constitution, are enshrined in the religious beliefs and practices of our Judeo-Christian foundations. Without an understanding of these ideas, values and principles, and without establishing a specific definition of 'secular', how can we ever truly understand Australia?

How does a 12 year-old understand Australia in the way the AC implies?

Perhaps there is another underlying purpose in the curriculum – one that comes from the left field. Is it possible, when all the layers have been peeled away, 'contemporary Australian society' is really only about being 'contemporary'?

Given that this definition is the current one, could it be the intention of the AC to encourage change to the Constitution – our 'set of rules' – via our students?

How well do you know the Australian Constitution – the Constitution our forefathers negotiated, made sacrifices and died for? If your answer is, 'Not very well', then don't be alarmed; you are not alone. And if you asked a typical 12-year-old the same question, chances are they'd be on the same page.

If you can't quite meet the Achievement Standard, then perhaps it's time to brush up on your knowledge of the Constitution.

First Published 17 July 2018

Chapter 8: Politics and Schools

Discrimination: Discerning Difference

Discrimination – the capacity to recognise a distinction or to differentiate – is a remarkable innate trait without which we could not survive. Babies are hard-wired to discriminate – to identify their mothers' features among those of other women. We discriminate between edible plants and toxic species to avoid poisoning. We discriminate between the features, traits and behaviours of prospective partners, so as to find love.

Despite its value, discrimination has come to be considered as the modern taboo. In what amounts to a contempt for our personal beliefs and qualities – and those we share – the 'anti-discrimination' movement has successfully created war among us. It demands everything be inclusive and the same. No-one is safe from its attacks, and its ultimate targets are history and religion. Christianity and Islam are both monotheistic religions, for example, but they are not the same.

Consider the following statements. Can you discriminate between those that are factual, those that are false (incorrect), and those that represent belief or opinion?

1. There is only one god.
2. All Christians believe the Eucharist contains the body, blood, soul and divinity of Christ.

Thought Starters On Education

3. The Hadith is a source of moral guidance and religious law that mirrors Christianity.
4. All women are pure.
5. The Sunnah and the Quran are teachings of Islam.
6. Queen Elizabeth I established the Church of England.
7. Marriage can include more than one wife.
8. The purpose of Islam is to reign supreme across the globe.
9. The Feudal Society was replaced by a money-based market economy.
10. The Sunnah is the primary source of Islamic Law (Sharia).
11. All men of the cloth are paedophiles.
12. There are many gods.

Schools actively teach discrimination using a strategy known as 'comparing and contrasting' – for instance, comparing and contrasting 'two', 'to' and 'too', or comparing and contrasting a character's traits at the beginning of a novel with those at the end.

But do schools themselves discriminate between materials in recommended texts or print media to enable the accurate teaching of religious and historical content? Can they effectively distinguish between truth and fabrication?

Chapter 8: Politics and Schools

We must never forget this fundamental principle: our nation was founded on Judeo-Christian values. Students must be taught how to discriminate, with absolute accuracy, between these values and those of any other religion.

Christianity and Islam are both religions, yet they are certainly not the same. God forbid our children would walk through any school gate into a world that cannot discriminate between the two.

First Published 9 July 2018

Thought Starters On Education

Faith in Morality

Public schools in Australia are widely referred to as offering a secular education, which, by definition, should not have a connection with religious or spiritual matters.

However, the singing of Christmas Carols and a strong emphasis on indigenous studies – including spirituality – is evident in many schools.

Curious to understand the origins of secular education better, I recently read *The First Report of the Commissioners of National Education for the Colony of Victoria for the year 1852*. It makes for fascinating reading.

A teacher should be a person of Christian sentiment, of calm temper and discretion; he should be imbued with a spirit of peace, of obedience to the law, and of loyalty to his sovereign.

The commissioners who were responsible for schools at the time devolved power to local communities, and also maintained that any school that wished to be part of National Education for the Colony of Victoria must maintain Christianity as an intrinsic value.

Here's a little of what the report includes:

- A copy of the following lesson be hung up in each school: "Christians should endeavour, as the Apostle Paul commands them, to 'live peaceably with all

Chapter 8: Politics and Schools

men' (Rom. Ch. xii. v. 17), even with those of a different religious persuasion".

- A teacher should be a person of Christian sentiment, of calm temper and discretion; he should be imbued with a spirit of peace, of obedience to the law, and of loyalty to his sovereign.
- If any other books than the Holy Scriptures...are employed in communicating religious instruction, each work is to be made known to the Local Patrons by the pastor or religious instructor...
- Opportunities and facilities are to be afforded to the children for receiving such religious instruction as their parents or guardians approve.
- The patrons of every school have the right of appointing such religious instruction as they may think proper to be given therein, provided that each school be open to children of all communion.

More important, it seems that secular education was never intended to ignore religion or faith, but rather to tackle the issue of land distribution for schools between Christian denominations. And we must not forget that early schooling was dominated by the social and moral needs of our early immigrants.

The report goes on to describe common instruction, teaching apprenticeships and annual examinations of teachers to determine their suitability for ongoing employment.

Thought Starters On Education

Today, some would argue that the referendum on same-sex marriage, the Royal Commission into Child Sexual Abuse in Religious and other organisations, or the increasing number of those practising Islam, are indications that Christianity is losing its way. I would argue that Christianity is under threat, and with it, our secular education, our public schools, and the social and moral fibre of our nation.

I would argue that Christianity is under threat, and with it, our secular education, our public schools, and the social and moral fibre of our nation.

Stumbling across *The First Report of the Commissioners of National Education for the Colony of Victoria for the year 1852* was fascinating reading for me. I would hope that this and other historical documents of similar significance become the light and the hope of maintaining and celebrating our Judeo/Christian foundations.

First Published 21 May 2018

Chapter 8: Politics and Schools

Safe Schools No More

Has the *National Safe Schools Framework* been sabotaged?

Schools are places of learning for students and also the workplace of teachers. Parents place their trust in schools, expecting a duty of care will be provided and their children educated to the highest possible standard.

In 2003 the Howard Government introduced the *National Safe Schools Framework* (NSSF). The aim was to provide an agreed national approach to help all schools and their communities address issues of bullying, harassment, violence and child abuse and neglect.

In 2010 the Gillard Government amended the NSSF. The same year, the Brumby Government in Victoria adopted the *Safe Schools Coalition* (SSC) program, which was based on La Trobe Universities *Gay and Lesbian Health Victoria* model. In 2013 the Rudd/Gillard Government provided $8 million dollars to assist the national rollout of the Victorian SSC program.

Despite the Howard Government's best intentions, the actions of Gillard/Rudd/Brumby made it impossible to protect children in public schools.

> *The Turnbull Government today*
> *is facing a similar challenge*

Thought Starters On Education

HERE ARE NINE REASONS WHY:

1. Education is a complex business

Federal and State legislation makes it difficult to understand who influences public policy and accountability in schools. For example, the *Gay, Lesbian and Transgender Act* 2003 – the *Legislation Act* 2001 affects the *Safe Schools Coalition* program by way of definitions and omission of definitions. For example, an individual can select gender identity for any given life situation.

2. State legislation undermines the Federal government's intentions

State Governments have responsibility for public schools. The Federal Government provides additional funding but they do not register operate or oversee public schools. A national initiative, as intended by the Howard Government was an equaliser across all schools. The Victorian Government is imposing the SSC program on its public schools.

3. Sexual preference is given priority over literacy

There are 1524 public schools in Victoria, only 207 of those schools are members of the *Safe Schools Coalition*. The Victorian Government has mandated every secondary public school to follow the *Safe Schools Coalition* program by 2018; making gender and sexual preference a priority over literacy, numeracy, wellbeing and other content areas of the Australian Curriculum.

Chapter 8: Politics and Schools

4. Teacher courses only qualify individuals as generalist teachers

Whilst the Victorian Government has chosen to mandate teacher training of the *Safe Schools Coalition* program, there is no mandated training for literacy, numeracy, counselling or psychology across all pre-service courses. At the completion of pre-service teacher training graduates have a qualification either as a generalist teacher or a content specific teacher. There are no subjects that qualify pre-service teachers to be psychologists or therapists. This puts teachers at risk when dealing with complex issues, such as abuse or bullying, which are beyond their vocational capacity and responsibility.

5. There is personal conflict between parent, teacher and principal

If principals and teachers do not agree with the *Safe Schools Coalition* program their professional judgement is compromised by its mandate. Even worse, if principals and teachers are also parents, they have no way of protecting their own children from the mandate. Their hands are tied.

6. Parents relinquish their child once they are inside the school grounds

According to state legislation, public school employees have the power to deny any parent access to their own child once their child is inside the school gate. Schools have the power to issue trespass notices and intervention orders.

Thought Starters On Education

In 2010 an inner Melbourne public school issued trespass warning notices and interim intervention orders against parents who were seeking clarification of changes made to their children's school curriculum. Parents could face the same problem if taking a stand against the *Safe School Coalition* program.

7. Parents can be held liable

If a parent attempts to prevent their child from participating in the mandated *Safe Schools Coalition* program, they are held financially liable for defending legal action that the school or the Department of Education may take. The school is protected financially by the Department of Education.

8. The program does not protect the safety of all children

The term *Safe Schools* implies a positive environment for all students. However, the *Safe Schools Coalition* program only provides training resources and advice about homophobic and transphobic bullying. The reality is that bullying is not limited to gender or sexual preference and in every school the bullied and the bully come in all shapes, sizes, ethnicities, intellects and level of ability.

9. Building a positive culture takes time

The delivery of a program takes place within a given time frame. The creation of a culture of respect, patience, awareness, responsibility, equity, compassion and friendship

Chapter 8: Politics and Schools

are achieved over time through interaction, mistakes and achievements.

In 2003 the Federal Government had a vision for Australia. It's now 2016 and the Victorian Government has another. It has funded, co-created and now mandated the *Safe Schools Coalition* program. If the Victorian Government is successful in implementing this mandate, all other states could follow. Allowing this to happen is allowing State Government ownership and control over your child. There is nothing safe about that.

What's next?

If the *Safe Schools Coalition* program is allowed to proceed in Victoria and other states follow, every public school in the Nation will be placing the *Safe Schools Coalition* program ahead of literacy, numeracy, wellbeing and equity. Independent and denominational schools are not at risk of the same possibility.

Five actions you can take

1. Speak to your child's school principal to learn whether they have joined the *Safe Schools Coalition* and voice your views. Find out about your child's school policies, school council viewpoints and call for a community meeting to discuss the implications of the *Safe Schools Coalition*

2. Speak to your children about what being safe and equity means.

Thought Starters On Education

3. Speak to your State and Federal members of parliament and voice your views.
4. Begin a respectful dialogue with family, friends and colleagues to find out the views of others.
5. Do some research. Begin with the *Gay, Lesbian and Transgender Act 2003*.

First Published 3 September 2016

Chapter 8: Politics and Schools

The Servants of Hopes and Dreams

Politicians serve the community. They represent people they don't usually know personally – faceless, nameless citizens and families – with their hopes and dreams.

Public school leaders also serve the community. However, for them, it isn't a community of the faceless and the nameless. These leaders usually know these people and their families – with their hopes and dreams.

Like politicians, public school leaders have power and influence. However, they must not be swayed by policies and the trends in the political landscape. They must remain impartial. Their role is to represent the hopes and dreams of the families they serve.

Increasingly, public school leaders throughout the world are becoming political advocates. They often breathe life into extremely dangerous social policy – whether deliberately or unwittingly. Some have even become part of the worldwide movement towards the demise of nurturing and the death of parenting.

"I think it is very important that we educate the children the best we can...about gender, about gender stereotypes. It is never too young to start."

This statement was made by a school leader in the United Kingdom. An experiment, approved by the school leader,

Thought Starters On Education

involved schoolchildren being 'gender-neutral' for a whole term. The purpose was to determine whether being gender-neutral could even out any disparities in children's confidence and abilities.

In Sweden, schools have introduced gender advisors. This move supports the nation's view that if something is institutionalised – in a school for example – it will automatically bring about change in society.

Scotland is introducing gender-neutral schools. The justification: to reduce bullying.

Public schools in Australia have provided teachers with workbooks containing descriptions of cancer as a consequence of sin, and a gift from God, and content stating people should 'die for their faith if necessary'.

Middle schools in the USA have students write the shahada, the Islamic declaration of faith, as part of their calligraphy practice. These same schools, however, fail to inform students that Islam does not maintain the separation between the political and religious spheres, as Christianity does.

Do these issues sound similar to, or replicate, what's happening in your local school? How well do you know your local school leader?

Public school leaders have power and influence – and rightly so. The important question is this: does their power

Chapter 8: Politics and Schools

nurture the hopes and dreams of the families they serve, or further their own political agenda?

First Published 10 September 2018

Thought Starters On Education

💬 The Consequence of Freedom

Personal freedom! It's one's power, or right, to act, speak, or think as one wants. It's a fundamental principle in many societies – past, present and, presumably, future.

Or is it compromised to some extent by the personal freedom of others?

Is it fair to suggest that one's power, or right, to act, speak or think as one wants, must come with boundaries? If so, what are they and from where do they come?

It's impossible to expect, demand or fulfil one's personal freedom, without acknowledging the other side of the scale – personal responsibility.

All choices have consequences. And our choices rarely have consequences whose effects are limited to ourselves. For individuals to succeed, for families to thrive, and for society to be harmonious, most of us realise that to enjoy personal freedom, we must accept personal responsibility.

What are our Personal freedoms and from where do our personal responsibilities come?

1. The spiritual sphere, or moral law

Faith, religion and spiritual loyalty and freedom have been with us for centuries. However, figures suggest they are in

Chapter 8: Politics and Schools

grave decline. In 1911, Australia held its first census for its 4.5 million residents. A total of 357 religious categories were acknowledged at the time.

Australia claims to be a religiously diverse nation. In the most recent (2016) census, responses indicated that only three religious categories were of significant influence – Christianity (52%), Islam (2.6%) and Buddhism (2.4%). 30% of Australians reported that they have no religion. Is this the same as saying 30% of Australia's population has no moral principles? Or could it be said that the origins of those principles are unknown or are of no worth?

2. The physical sphere, or natural science

The natural environment is the genesis of all life. Our very existence is the result of two fundamental, unique powers, which are of equal importance, yet vastly different: mother earth and father sky. The giving of life is not achieved with 2 eggs; neither is it achieved with two sperm. Our very existence is impossible unless egg and sperm combine. 'How do we determine where we can exercise our human right to intervene, and where we must respect nature's right to protect and endure?'

3. The political sphere, or civil society

How is resolution to be achieved when one's own freedom is affected by the freedom of others? How does society determine the outcome when there is conflict between one freedom and another? Society survives because there is an overarching set of principles or laws by which everyone abides. Its members must live by the agreed rules of the game of life. Personal responsibility must be regarded as being of equal importance as personal freedom.

4. The economic sphere, or the exchange of benefits in business and personal life

To exchange is to give, to another, that which they do not have, with the full understanding that you will receive that which you do not have. Is receiving without giving a rejection of personal responsibility? To exchange is to honour difference and to acknowledge the things we are capable of, and those we are not.

Personal freedom! It's about the power or right to act, speak, or think as one wants. It's a fundamental principle of society – past, present and future. So too is personal responsibility.

In whom or what do you have complete faith? Are you guided by religious, physical, political or economic principles? How far are you prepared to go to maintain your personal freedom?

More importantly, in whom or what do you have complete faith? Or trust to be responsible for you, when your personal freedom has gone?

First Published 16 April 2016

Chapter 8: Politics and Schools

Dental Decay: Something is Rotten in the State of Victoria

Elections. They bring promises and disappointments at best, and divisiveness at worst.

The tag line for the Labor Party's campaign in Victoria was 'Delivering for all Victorians'.

The closing statement in the Victorian Premier's victory speech was 'The next four years will be about delivering for all Victorians'.

A clever campaign, and perhaps one that deserves congratulations for such a clean and obvious message. But that's where the promises end and the divisiveness begins.

Labor has pledged $396.8 million dollars to enable every State school student to receive dental care.

According to the Summary Statistics for Victorian Schools – July 2018, the number of students enrolled in public schools who will benefit from this promise is 618,846. If you do the sums, that's $642 per public school student in one year.

The remaining 352,822 students in Catholic and Independent schools, as well as the unaccounted-for home schooled

Thought Starters On Education

students, are apparently not worthy of the same dental health care as that promised to public school students.

This is not 'delivering for all Victorians'.

Although many questions could be raised regarding the socio-economic status of Victorian families, and the assumption that only the disadvantaged attend public schools, this is not the fundamental issue.

What needs to asked is this:

Why is funding for dental health tied to public schools?

The average Victorian is not covered by the basic dental services proposed under this pledge. Tying $396.8 million dollars in dental services only to children attending public schools does not equate to 'delivering for all Victorians'.

Elections bring promises and disappointments at best, and divisiveness at worst.

The latest, and not the least of these, is the Victorian government's self-serving obsession with power at the expense of education, principals, teachers and Victorian families in general.

First Published 26 November 2018

Chapter 8: Politics and Schools

What Is This Space We Call Place?

Schools deliver what is known as the intended curriculum. This includes broad, written statements that reflect what students should know, understand, and be able to do, by the end of each school year. It sets a framework of expectations or standards with regard to what all students should be taught – regardless of where they live or what their circumstances might be. It is intended to ensure a degree of consistency across all schools.

How familiar are you with the intended curriculum? How well do you know what your child is being taught? Or, if you are an educator, how well do you know the curriculum you are expected to deliver?

Parents and teachers should have a sound understanding of the intended curriculum if they are to accept its content or voice concern over its intent. This begins with an understanding of the definitions and interpretations hidden within the curriculum.

Here's an example of what I mean:

'In the Australian Curriculum, Country, or Place, refers to a space mapped out by physical or intangible boundaries that individuals or groups of Aboriginal Peoples occupy and regard as their own'.

Thought Starters On Education

Do you know what spaces with intangible boundaries look like? This statement is written in the curriculum for students at Foundation level. In other words, five-year-olds are taught this, and should, therefore, be able to explain physical and intangible boundaries.

And, according to the Australian Curriculum, 'visible elements of a place… are replaced by the term characteristics, which includes both visible and invisible elements of a place'.

Could this be interpreted to mean that Aboriginal Peoples occupy, and regard as their own, all Australian soil and all characteristics of it?

I'm sure this isn't the case. However, it highlights the need for our understanding of what is being taught.

What's more, to achieve this understanding requires a genuine relationship between parent and teacher. Otherwise, what is intended could be misrepresented and misunderstood: the result of which would be to mislead an entire generation.

And then, which 'intangible boundary' or 'invisible element' would determine our education?

First published 4 June 2018

www.ingramcontent.com/pod-product-compliance
Lightning Source LLC
Chambersburg PA
CDIIW071910200106
44110CB00013B/1400